CRAFT PRODUCTION AND TRADE IN SOUTH KANARA

CRAFT PRODUCTION AND TRADE in South Kanara : A.D. 1000-1763

Nagendra E. Rao

GYAN PUBLISHING HOUSE
New Delhi - 110002

The Publication of this book has been financially supported by the Indian Council of Historical Research. The Responsibility for the facts stated or opinions expressed is entirely of the author and not of the council.

Craft Production and Trade in South Kanara
A.D.(1000-1763)

ISBN : 81-212-0916-1

Published in 2006 in India by
Gyan Publishing House,
5, Ansari Road, Daryaganj,
New Delhi-110002
Phones: 23282060, 23261060,
Fax. 23285914
email : books@gyanbooks.com
Website : www.gyanbooks.com

Laser Type Setting by: Mega Graphics, Delhi
Printed at: Salasar Imaging System, Delhi

Contents

Acknowledgements

The present study would not have taken this shape without the active support of many individuals and institutions. First and foremost, I express my deep sense of gratitude to Dr. N. Shyam Bhat, Reader, Department of History, Goa University. I thank him for the guidance and encouragement given throughout the course of this work.

I am grateful to my teachers, Prof. B. Surendra Rao, Chairman, Department of History, Mangalore University, and Prof. Kesavan Veluthat, Department of History, Mangalore University, for their valuable suggestions. I am indebted to my uncle, Dr. K. G. Vasanthamadhava, Pavanje, and Dr. A. K. Shastri, Sirsi, who were kind enough to allow me to refer some of the rare and valuable documents and *kadatas* in their personal collections.

I thank my colleagues - Dr. K. M. Mathew, formerly, Professor and Head, Dr. Pratima P. Kamat, Head, Dr. Pius Malekandathil, Sri Ujjayan Bhattacharya and Sri Venugopalan Nair - in the Department of History, Goa University, for their co-operation and encouragement. I also acknowledge the support that I received from my friends.

I thank the authorities of Goa University for providing me the facilities to work for my Ph.D Degree. The minor research project sanctioned to me by the University on "Urbanization in Western Coastal India 1336-1763" enabled me to probe deeper into this area of economic history of South Kanara.

I am indebted to the authorities and staff of various institutions like Goa University Library, Historical Archives of Goa, Mysore University Library, Epigraphy Office, Mysore, Mangalore University Library, Karnatak University Library, Bombay University Library and Maharastra State Archives, Mumbai, for their help.

I thank my parents and family members, particularly my wife, Mrs. Shailaja Rao, for their whole-hearted support in the completion of this work.

I also thank the ICHR for the publication grant which has facilitated the publication of this book.

Place : Taleigao Plateau, Goa.

Date : April 2006 **Nagendra E. Rao**

Glossary

Acal: Variety of rice

Achari: Artisan

Accu Kottariya gadde: Land of artisan

Adake: Arecanut

Adikasu: Markets

Agasaru: Washer men

Aitihyas: Traditional narratives

Aliya Santana: Matrilineal system of inheritance typical to South Kanara. It is prevalent among a community called Bunts.

Anchu: Raised path between fields

Angadi: Shops

Ashrafis: Currnecy used in Portuguese India

Badagiya bayala gadde: Land of carpenter

Bahars: Weight

Barakanura Ghatta: Barkut ghat

Basadis : Jaina temples

Balanju: Trade guild

Balegara: Bangle seller

Bazaar: Market place

Bella: Jaggery

Cartazes : Sailing permits

Chaityalaya: Jaina religious structure

Chamaraseve: Worship with fans conducted in temples

Chikku: Sapota

Chinambara: Silk cloth

Cuzados: Portuguese currency

Darsana: connected with religion
Devalaya: Temple
Doni: Log boats
Elamegalu: Trade guild
Ellu: Sesamum indicum
Estado da India: Portuguese India
Gadyanas: Currency
Gallivat: Boat with oars and triangular sail
Gana: Oil mill
Ganada sunki: Tax on oil
Gavares: Community of traders
Gavudas : measure of distance
Girasal: Variety of rice
Gramapramukhas: Elders of village
Gulama: Slave
Hadi: forest
Hagalu: Daytime
Halaru: Trade guilds
Halasu: Jack fruit
Hanate: Earthern lamp
Hanjamana: Trade guild
Harigolu: Skin boat
Heru: Load
Hesaru: Green gram
Hobalis: Administrative divisions
Hoi gana: Oil mill worked with bull
Honnus: Gold or gold coin
Horahinavaru : Outsiders
Jambukhana: Carpet
Jatres: Festival Markets

Jedarava: Weaver
Kabitas : Poems
Kadali: Banana
Kadatas : Account books
Kalase: Measure
Kallukuttigas: Stone sculptors
Kanchugaras: Bronze workers
Kammara kodage: Irrigation works
Kammara salu: Street of blacksmiths
Kattes: Rest houses
Keri: Street
Khandi: Weight
Kaifiyats : Record of traditional histories
Karbotigare: Blacksmiths
Kari kabbu: Black sugarcane
Kai gana: Oil mill worked with hand
Karkhanas: work shops
Katigadyanas: Currency
Kuliyalugalu: Hired labourers
Kumbaras: Potters
Kumbaradere: Tax imposed on potters
Kumbaragarike: Work of potters
kumbara hakala vivara: Property of potters
Madivala bettu : Land of washer men
Mahanagara: Great city
Maletharu: Land granted to garland makers
Mana: Weight
Manigaras: Traders in precious stones
Manigramam: Trade guild
Mathas: Religious institutions

Maunds: Weight
Mavu: Mango
Mente: Fenugreek
Mora: measure
Mudes: Measure of agricultural produce
Mukhamantapa: Front portion of temple
Muladalugalu : Bonded labourers
Mummuri-danda: Association of traders
Nadu: Agrarian territories
Nagaram: Commercial centres
Nagarasamuha: Town administrators
Nakhara-hanjamana: Trade guild
Nakhara-parivara: Association of traders
Nanadesis: Trade guild
Nanda divige: Perpetual lamp
Nangalla: Anchor
Nashta: Loss
Navigada prabhu: Lord of ships
Nishkas: Coin
Odari: Potter
Olagadavaru: Musicians
Oni: Narrow path
Pachade: Cloth
Pachary: Variety of rice
Paddanas : Folk songs
Padinentu pattana: Eighteen towns
Pagodas: Currency
Palli: Village or mosque
Panams: Currency
Panchavadya: Music in the temple

Paradesi: Foreign

Parao: Large vessels

Patta: Cloth

Pattanaswami: Lord of Towns

Patsalis: Silk weavers

Pattasaliga: Silk weaver

Pauju: Army

Pethe: Market place

Poorva mariyade: Ancient usage

Pura: Town

Puttige: Basket

Quavages: Variety of rice

Rajas: Chieftains

Rajabidi: Main road

Rajya: State or territory

Saleyavaru: Weavers

Salike: Business in a room or shop

Salikeya ballalugalu: Members of guild of businessmen

Samastha kattale: Traditional law

Samsthana: Territory belonging to state or religious institution

Santhes: Markets

Sasana: Order

Seers: Measure

Settis : Traders

Settikaras: Trade guilds

Simes: Administrative divisions

Sitalamalige: Wear house

Sribali: Type of religious ceremony in temples

Sthalapuranas : Local traditional stories

Sthalaśenabhovike: Administration of locality

Sunkathanes: Custom stations

Svadesi: Indigenous

Svamya: Ownership

Tanes: Custom stations

Tattirayas: Wooden figures used in temple festivals

Teji: Horse

Teppa: Raft

Tupaki: Rifle

Tuppa: Ghee

Uddu: Phaseolus mungo

Umbali: Land grant

Ubhayananadesis: Trade guild

Uppina kavali: Salt pans

Vinimaya vartakasangha: Exchange trade guilds

Visa: Currency

Vishaya: Administrative division

Xerafins: Portuguese coins

1
Introduction

This book deals with the empirical and analytical study of the system of craft production and trade in South Kanara from A.D.1000 to 1763. As in the earlier period of its history, during this phase too South Kanara continued to exist predominantly as an agrarian economy. However, there existed considerable craft production or industrial activity which drew sustenance from agriculture. In fact agriculture and agrarian-based craft production thrived as the two major pillars of the economy of this region. The flourishing agrarian economy and the surplus production in the primary sector created conditions favourable for the development of industries, industrial production and trade. Trade was carried out in both agricultural and industrial products. This included inland trade, and sea trade between various regions in the country as well as with countries like Persia and others. Though traditionally barter system prevailed, during this period money economy came into being and both continued to exist side by side.

Political changes and administrative policies affected the system of production (both agricultural and industrial) and trade. Political changes in the region such as the fall of the Alupas, rise and fall of the Hoysalas, Vijayanagara and Keladi and the impact of these on the economy, production and trade are considered here. The society was organised and hierarchically arranged on the basis of the caste system. Caste determined the work or profession of the individual and in many cases their settlements too. The relations between caste, craft production and trade are analysed. Similarly religion and religious institutions like temples and *mathas* were important in the development of trade and trading centres.

The arrival of foreign traders, Persians, Arabs, Portuguese

and others, and the emergence of various ports and port towns like Basrur, Kundapur, Gangolli, Barkur, Baindur, Malpe, Mulki, Mangalore, Kumbla, etc. and trade routes are important in this study. In the same way, the various factors which led to the process of urbanisation and economic transformation are examined.

Sources

The sources for the present study are copious. They include primary sources, published and unpublished, and secondary sources. They are inscriptions, *kadatas*, English, Portuguese and Dutch records, travelogues and folklore. There are also sources like *Kaifiyats, sthalapuranas* and legends which could be used carefully along with corroboratory evidences. Besides these, a large number of published works, both in English and Kannada could be used for an analysis of the data on South Kanara in a better and broader historical perspective.

Inscriptions give authentic information regarding various aspects of history. Many inscriptions of South Kanara throw light on craft production, trade, traders, markets, etc. Most of them belong to the period from 8th century to 17th century A.D. They are identified and published in the ***Mysore Archaeological Reports***[1], ***Epigraphia Carnatica***[2], ***Epigraphia Indica***[3], ***Karnataka Inscriptions***[4] and ***South Indian Inscriptions,***[5] Volume VII and Volume IX Part I and II. Besides these, there are many unpublished inscriptions which are discovered and used by scholars like P. Gururaja Bhatt, K.V. Ramesh, K.G. Vasanthamadhava, B. Vasantha Shetty and others. We have utilised the data available in these inscriptions by referring to the works of these scholars.

Kadatas form another major category of original sources used here. *Kadatas* or black books are unpublished Kannada records. These are written by the court writers on the command of the rulers. They generally deal with the topics like sale and purchase of land, accounts of the business families, accounts of trade, etc. These are found in the custody of some private individuals and also in the Karnataka State Archives, Bangalore, where they are microfilmed and preserved. Some of the *kadatas* are like unpublished account books and give details of internal trade of the region. A few others refer to the different communities like goldsmiths, potters and other craftsmen. In the *kadatas* there are references to *karkhanas* (work shops) where there was the production of goods which were purchased by both the traders as well as the people by directly approaching the producers. They also inform the prices of goods like rice, jaggery, coconut, arecanut, grocery and other items.

Some of the English documents preserved in the Maharashtra State Archives, Mumbai, are useful for the present study. They include volumes of Public Department Diary, Carwar Factory Outward Letter Book, Secretariat Inward Letter Book and Secretariat Outward Letter Book. The series of volumes edited by William Foster under the title ***English Factories in India***[6] furnish important data regarding trade activities in South Kanara.

The Portuguese sources furnish much information on their activities in the Asian ports. They provide quantitative data which are very useful to know the system of weights and measures, factories, volume of trade, fluctuations in trade due to intervention or changing political relations or market conditions of the state and the trading communities of South Kanara. For example, the *Livro do Cartazes*[7] mentions the ships of traders of South Kanara, quantity of goods traded by them, places where they traded and commodity composition. Similarly, *Livro do Correspondencia do Kanara* [8] is also a very useful document for the present study. There are certain Portuguese works like ***Archivo Portuguese Oriental***[9], ***Asia Portuguesa***[10] and ***Collecçao de Tratados e Concertos de Pazes....***[11] P.S.S. Pissurlencar edited works like ***Agentes da Diplomacia Portuguesa na India***[12], ***Regimentos das Fortalezas da India***[13], ***Assentos do Conselho do Estado***[14]. F. C. Danvers wrote the work, ***Report of the Portuguese Records Relating to the East Indies***[15]. These works are useful to reconstruct the Portuguese commercial activities in South Kanara.

The Dutch records used by us are in the form of translations of a few pages from the *Dagh Register* which are given in the Journals of Bombay Historical Society.[16]

Accounts of foreign travellers constitute a major source of information for this study. The activities of Jewish traders are recorded by S.D. Goitien in his ***Letters of Jewish Traders.*** [17] The notices of the Arab travellers on South Kanara are seen from the work, ***The Knowledge of India Possessed by Arab Geographers Down to the 14th Century A.D. With Special Reference to Southern India***[18]. This book covers the views of Arab travellers like Abul Fida, Ferishta, Yaqut and Damishqi regarding the trade centres of South Kanara. It is said that Mangalore was one of the biggest trade centres in the Malabar coast.[19] The views of Ibn Batuta can be seen in the book ***Travels in Asia and Africa.***[20] Ibn Batuta described the land route from Kanara to Malabar.[21] To him Mangalore was a place where pepper and ginger were available in large quantity.[22]

The Book of Duarte Barbosa[23] edited by Mansel Longworth deals with aspects like the status of the province of Tulunadu which was a part of Vijayanagara, ports of South Kanara, their geographical location and importance. ***The Suma Oriental*** of Tom Pires[24] provides information on the trading activities in the ports of Kanara. Pietro Della Valle[25] noticed the political developments and described the relations between the native chieftains of South Kanara, the Keladi rulers and the Portuguese. H.L.Nage Gowda edited the volumes of ***Pravasi Kanda India*** (in Kannada).[26] They provide the accounts of foreign travellers like Nicolo Conti, Dom Duarte Menezes, Pyrard Delaval, Linschoten, Tom Pires, Thomas Herbert, Mandel Sella, John de Tevno and others.

Alexander Hamilton's work ***A New Account of the East Indies***[27] informs us about the trade between Basrur and Muscat.

From Muscat the traders brought horses, dates, pearl and other merchandise of the products of Arabia to South Kanara. He also speaks about the trade routes between South Kanara and other regions.

The Travels of Abbe Carre in India and the Near East [28] bears testimony to the existence of the English trading agency in Kanara as early as 1672. Further it mentions the trading links between Mangalore, Persia and Arabia. ***The Voyage of John Huyghen Van Linschoten to the East Indies*** [29] gives an account of the trading activities in the ports of South Kanara. His work is particularly useful to understand the competition between European powers like the Portuguese, English and Dutch. Ludovico de Varthema left his accounts in ***Itinerario***[30]. He mentions about the existence of craft producers in the bazaar of 'Olala'.[31] Francis H. Buchanan's ***Journey From Madras Through the Countries of Mysore, Canara and Malabar***[32] gives useful information on the different communities, agricultural and craft production.

Another category of source available for the present study is folklore. The folklore of South Kanara consists of *paddanas*, *kabitas,* legends and proverbs. The *paddanas* are anthologies which are sung by the agriculturists and mostly these are related to the religious life of the people. *Paddanas* give details on the day to day life of the people. They refer to the different communities producing agricultural and craft goods. Places of production and trading centres are mentioned in them. *Kabitas* are poems sung by people and they refer to their living condition. *Aitihyas* or legends are traditional stories or narratives which could be used only with the support of reliable historical data. Proverbs describe the attitude of the people towards different professional communities like artisans and traders.

Some of the Kannada literary works can be used for the present study. Kavi Chandrama wrote ***Gomatesvara Charitre***[33] which describes the different streets of Karkal and gives references to artisanal and trading activities. ***Linganna Kavi's Keladi Nripa Vijayam***[34] helps in studying the relations between the Chieftains of South Kanara and the Keladi rulers. It also refers to the activities of the Portuguese in South Kanara.

Geographical Setting

According to the tradition, Parashurama ksetra[35] is known for the fertility of soil, abundant rainfall and wealth.[36] South Kanara has a variety of flora and fauna. It has mountains, valleys, rivers and ports. South Kanara has Arabian sea as its western boundary. This coast line is about 80 miles. It is almost straight, but in some places it is broken with rivers, rivulets, small streams, etc. The Western ghats are situated on the eastern side of the District. Some of the peaks in the ghats rise about 6000 feet above than the sea level. The average altitude of the ghats is about 2000 feet. This has separated the coastal strip from the upghat regions of Karnataka. It made large scale contact between the two regions difficult till modern roads and transport system developed. However, there was no total isolation of South Kanara from the rest of Karnataka. From early times, these contacts were established through the routes of Kollur, Hosangadi, Agumbe, Shiradi and Sampaje ghats. North Kanara and Kerala are situated to the north and south of South Kanara respectively.

The rivers of South Kanara run from the east to the west. With the heavy rainfall of south-west monsoon and the broken nature of the country, the rivers and streams are innumerable. Since the volume of water is very great at times, they do not facilitate transportation. In the dry weather, owing to rocky character of their beds, the rivers are not usually navigable. However, within these limits they are very extensively used for bringing products to the coastal ports and towns. The backwaters and salt water lagoons provide great facilities for traffic.[37]

The principal rivers of South Kanara are Netravati,

Gurupur, Gangolli, Sitanadi and Suvarnanadi. The Netravati originates in the ghats to the east of Kudremukh and flows down the Bangadi valley. At Uppinangadi it meets another larger river called Kumaradhare which comes from Kumara Parvata near Subrahmanya. From Bantwal onwards the river is navigable to boats of a capacity of 3 tons and as it approaches Mangalore, the channel assumes wider proportions.

Gangolli river consists of several streams which fall into the sea at Gangolli. Haladi is navigable even at the driest season by boats containing one *corji* or about 1½ tons of rice. Chakranadi is navigable for boats of small burthen as far as Wandse.

The Sitanadi takes its rise in the ghats beyond Someshwar to the north-east of Udupi taluk, while the Suvarnanadi flows from the hills situated at south-eastern boundary of the same taluk. Both fall into the sea at Barkur or Hangarakatta, nearly eight miles to the north of the town of Udupi and a large backwater being formed by their junction. The Sitanadi is navigable as far as Kokkarne, 11 miles inland. The Suvarnanadi is navigable upto Baje about 12 miles from the coast.[38] The above survey shows that South Kanara consists of some important rivers which on the one hand facilitated transport and on the other provided fertile land for agricultural production.

Nature of the Economy

Being located on the western coast, South Kanara had the advantage of several ports. The ports of South Kanara are mentioned in the writings of Greco-Roman scholars. Pliny and Ptolemy mention the trade centre Nitrias and Nitra respectively. This can be identified with a town located on the banks of Netravati river, namely, Mangalore. The Roman scholar Arrian in his book *Indica* called Mangalore as Mandegora. A 6th century work, *Christian Topography* by Kosmos Indikopluestes mentioned Mangarout.[39] One second century Greek drama mentioned the port of Udyavara.[40] The

Alupas ruled from the beginning of the Christian era to the fourteenth century. Udyavara was their capital and it was a flourishing trade centre till 12th century A.D. The Udyavara inscription of Chitravahana II mentions the cities of Udyavar and Mangalore.[41] The Udyavara inscription of Prathvisagara which belongs to 9th century A.D. mentions that custom duties were collected both in land routes and water transport. The king donated half of the custom duty to the Patti Pombuccha Nagara. For this he had to take the permission of traders of Udyavara.[42] This reveals that Udyavara and Patti Pombuccha had trade connections and that in Udyavara the traders organised themselves into guilds. Vijayaditya's Udyavara inscription also mentions that half of the tax collected was given to the city of Patti Pombuccha. This inscription mentions about *nakharadavaru*[43] of Udyavara.[44]

Another inscription[45] mentions the following taxes that were collected by the state:

Item	*Tax*
2 ½ bags of grain	1 ½ *puttige*(basket) of grain
1 *mana* cotton	16 *pala* cotton
1 *heru*(load) arecanut	300 arecanut
1 *heru* chilly	16 *pala* chilly

The above details show the kind of craft production and trade that existed till the end of the 10th century A.D. The major trade centres of this period were Udyavara, Patti Pombuccha and Mangalore. There was the existence of towns, traders and trade guilds. Sources indicate the existence of regional trade. In the historical period, Barkur, Basrur and Mangalore were the important ports. New Mangalore harbour continues to be the rendezvous of South Kanara today.

The economy of South Kanara was predominantly agricultural in nature. The surplus production in the primary sector led to the development of trade. Thus the agrarian production catered to the needs of the natives and met the demand from outside. P. Gururaja Bhat stated that South Kanara in the pre-modern period was essentially an agricultural district and 75% of the population depended for their livelihood on cultivation.[46] Land was divided into rice and garden lands. The garden lands consisted of coconut and arecanut plantations. It is said that 22 kinds of agricultural implements were used.[47]

The brahmans, their *agraharas* and temples were the prominent land owners of South Kanara. The brahmanical tradition, *Gramapaddhati,* speaks about the existence of 32 brahmana villages. It is suggested that these villages were situated on the river valleys and fertile zones of the western coast.[48] The land was granted to temples and brahmans by the kings and traders. This enhanced significantly the economic position of the brahmans in South Kanara.[49]

There were merchants who tried to own land. K.V.Ramesh stated that organisations such as *Settikaras*[50] and *Halaru*[51] guilds and the *Mahajanas* also owned land in their collective capacity.[52] The inscriptions refer to *Halara gadi*[53] and *halaru* as land owners.[54] The artisans mostly owned non-agrarian lands which could not be cultivated.[55] We find reference to *madivala bettu* or land of washermen, *bestara bettu* or land of fishermen, *kumbara adi* or land of potters.[56] But there are also references to artisans who owned cultivable land. For example, we come across phrases like *badagiya bayala gadde* and *Accu Kottariya gadde*.[57]

These land owners cultivated only a part of their land and leased out much of their land to the tenants for cultivation and collected a part of the produce from them. Sometimes they hired labourers (*kuliyalugalu*), and also used bonded labourers (*muladalugalu*) for the purpose of cultivation.[58] We do not get much information regarding the agrarian relation and the ratio in which agricultural produce was shared.

Some of the chief agricultural products included rice,

coconut, arecanut, horse-gram, black-gram, ragi, gingily, pepper, cardamom, chillies, sugar-cane, tobacco, betel-leaf, castor, turmeric, cotton and ginger. The Mudubidre copper plate inscription of Chauta Abbakkadevi refers to coconut plantations.[59] Coconuts were grown not only for domestic consumption but also to export on large scale. Sometimes coconut gardens were leased out for cultivation.[60] *Adake* or arecanut was another profitable cash crop. An inscription from Basrur refers to taking of areca tree in procession to a temple.[61] Other crops produced were *savute* and other vegetables, *mavu* (mango), *halasu* or jack, *kadali* (one variety of banana) and *chikku* (sapota)[62] Most of the peasants were sudras. However there are references to some brahmanical groups which participated in agricultural pursuit.[63]

The above survey shows that agriculture was the major occupation of the people in South Kanara. Craft production or industries remained subordinate to agriculture. Obviously people largely depended on agriculture for their livelihood. Craft production was agro-based in nature and it brought revenue to the artisans. Agriculture and industries were interdependent because agriculture provided raw materials required for craft production such as coir, jaggery, sugar, etc. The land owners and labourers undertook artisan activities also and they could devote more time when they did not have much work in their fields. The traders traded both in agricultural and industrial goods. Many of the traders (*Settis*) belonged to the agricultural community and they carried out both these activities simultaneously. Trade and the resultant profit led to increased wealth and accumulation of capital. This enhanced the economic and social status of traders. Most of the artisans lived in the rural areas and did not migrate in large scale to the urban centres.

Political Background

The political history of South Kanara, beginning from the 7th century A.D. to the conquest of the region in 1763 by Haidar Ali of Mysore, saw the rule of the Alupas, the kings of Vijayanagara and the Nayakas of Keladi. The Alupas who

South Kanara during the Alupa period

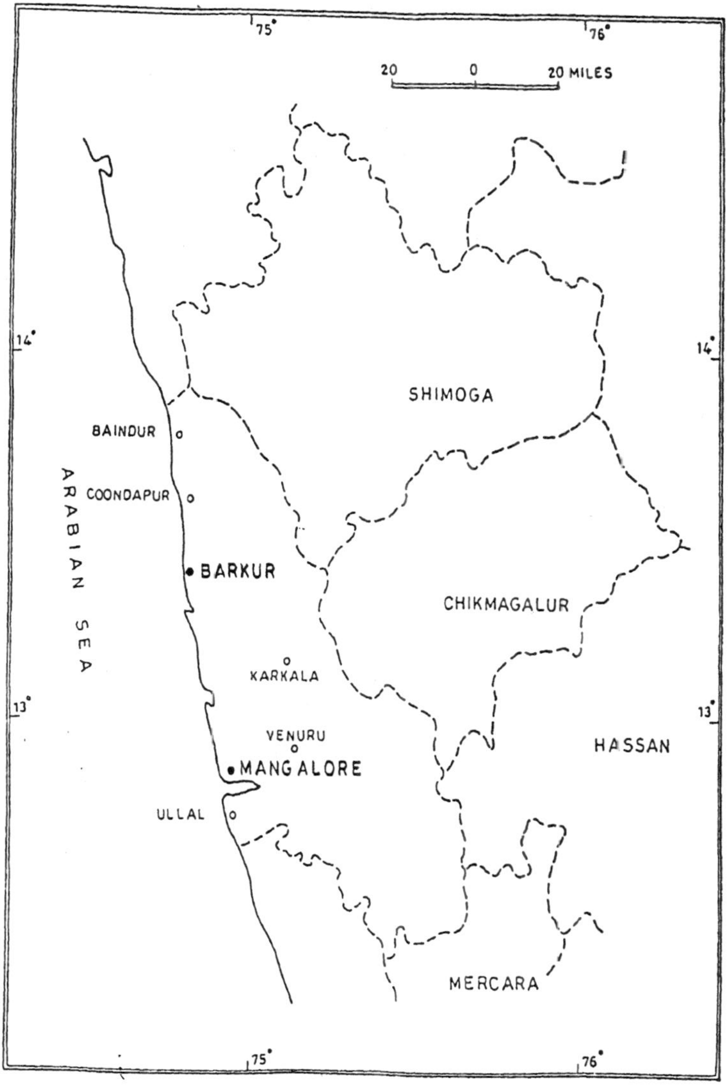

ruled as the feudatories of the different ruling dynasties of Karnataka such as the Chalukyas of Badami, the Rashtrakutas of Malkhed, the Chalukyas of Kalyana and the Hoysalas of Dwarasamudra had South Kanara under their control till the end of the 14th century. Mangalore, Udyavara and Barkur were the political centres of the Alupas at various periods of history. During the rule of Vijayanagara (c. 1345 A.D. to 1550), the Governors were the connecting link between the Empire and South Kanara. There were two *rajyas*, namely Mangalore and Barkur, each under a Governor. The kings of Vijayanagara gave considerable importance to South Kanara, for, its ports - Barkur, Basrur, Mangalore, etc.- facilitated trade and brought revenue to the Government.

By 1554 South Kanara came under the control of the Keladi rulers. It was a part of their kingdom until 1763. In that year Haidar Ali conquered Bidanur and along with that annexed the coastal districts of Karnataka to his kingdom.

During the last days of the Alupa rule and in the immediate post-Alupa period (between the 12th and 15th centuries), there came into existence a number of local ruling families in South Kanara. They were the Savantas of Mulki (c. 1411 to 1700), the Choutas of Ullal or Mudabidre (c. 1160-1801), the Bhairarasa Odeyas of Karkal (c. 1240 to 1650), the Ajilas of Venur (c. 1418 to 1800), the Tolaharas of Surala (c. 1139 to 1800), the Bangas of Bangadi or Bangavadi (c. 1410 to 1800), the Rajas of Kumbla (c. 12th century to 1800), and the Rajas of Vittal (c. 1436 to 1800). The territory of the *Rajas* of Nileshwar was annexed to South Kanara in 1737, and they too continued their rule up to 1800. These local chieftains except the *Rajas* of Nileshwar, continued to enjoy their position as the feudatories of the Vijayanagara, Keladi and Mysore rulers. The Nileshwar *Rajas* ruled under the Keladi and Mysore rulers.[64]

After the 15th century, Europeans like the Portuguese, Dutch and the English arrived in South Kanara and they tried to establish their factories in ports like Mangalore, Basrur

South Kanara under the Vijayanagara empire

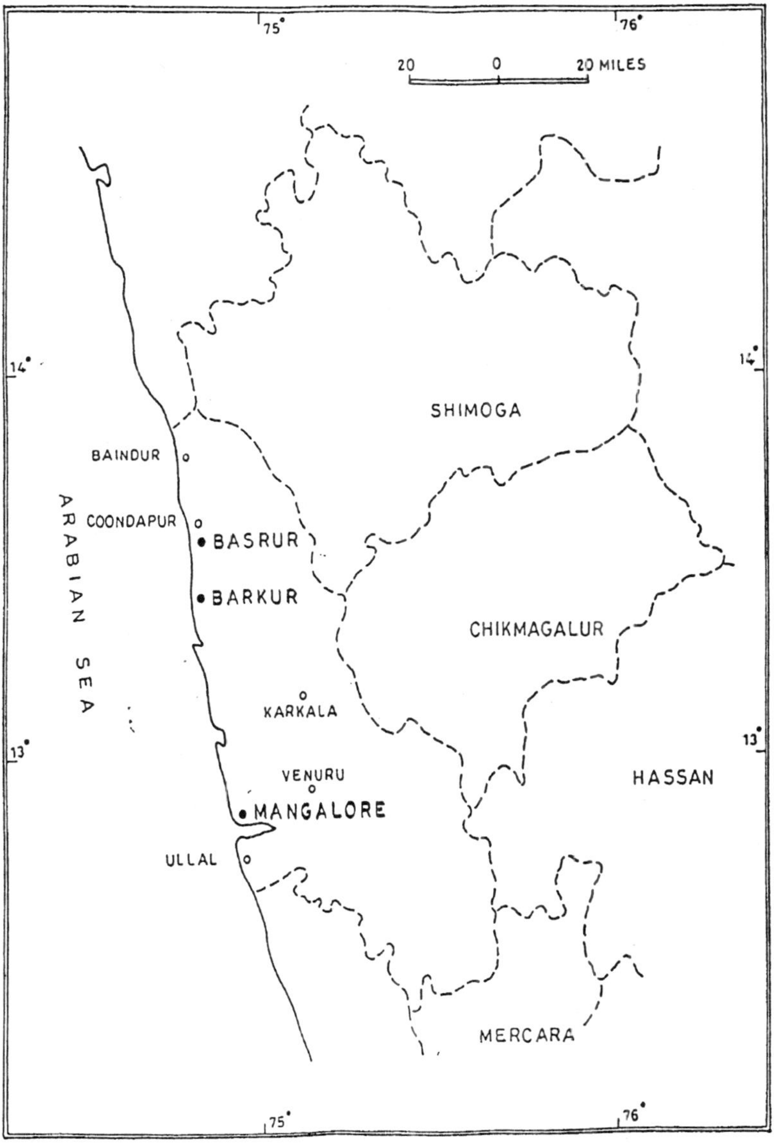

and Gangolli. The European element considerably influenced the economy, trade and commerce of South Kanara. The Portuguese signed treaties with the native rulers and tried to obtain supply of necessary provisions to their factories in different parts of India and abroad. During this interaction there were military encounters and political negotiations. This led to proliferation of trade in items like rice, pepper, ginger, iron, saltpetre, etc. The Dutch and the English attempted to compete with the Portuguese. The Dutch established their factories in Mangalore and Basrur. The English also appointed their agents in Mangalore to procure necessary supplies of rice to their settlements in Tellicherry and Bombay.

The above survey of the political history shows that there were significant changes in the political scenario in South Kanara during the period of our study. The changes in political scene affected the economy as well. While agriculture prospered, industrial activities could not grow well due to the absence of continued patronage. Further these changes did not affect trade adversely as almost all rulers showed interest in its promotion as it brought revenue to the state. The rule of the kings of Vijayanagara and Keladi led to expansion of trade. The contact with Europeans further expanded the trade network of South Kanara. Now the traders of South Kanara took part both in coastal trade and long distance overseas trade.

Nature and Scope

This book attempts to study the history of craft production and trade in South Kanara from A.D. 1000 to 1763 A.D. Both original and secondary sources in different languages are used. These data on the history of South Kanara are analysed and used by us as far objectively as possible and in a broader historical perspective. For this purpose we have consulted notable publications in the area of economic history. Statistics available on production, trade, etc. are used and presented in the book. The statistical data enabled us to prove our arguments in the areas of industrial

South Kanara during the Kelad period

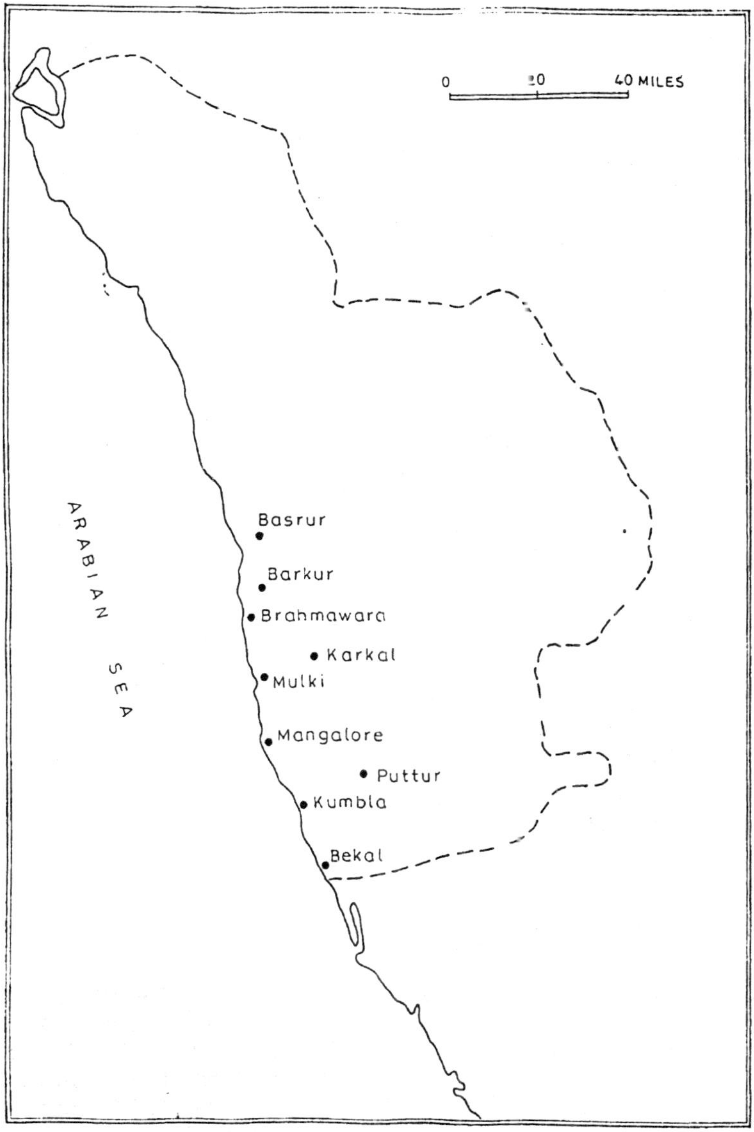

production, trade, migration and urbanisation. The dynamics of craft production, artisan communities, production centres and their products, guilds, etc. are examined. In the field of trade, both agricultural and non-agricultural goods are considered. This had to be so due to the dominant agrarian character of the economy of South Kanara. We have included trade in spices as well as victuals. In other words, both 'big trade' and 'small trade' are examined. Most of the economic activities had to be analysed in the context of a caste-stratified society. The socio-economic transformation of the region due to the growth of trade, the process of urbanisation and emergence of socio-economic elites are considered. The role of the state, rulers, merchants, temples and *mathas* and the influential classes of the society is studied.

1000 A.D. is taken as the starting point due to the availability of ample sources from this period onwards. It was after A.D.1000 that more changes could be seen in the economy of South Kanara. The year 1763 marked the fall of Nayakas of Keladi and the annexation of South Kanara to the Mysore kingdom by Haidar Ali.

Notes and References

1. ***Mysore Archaeological Report***, Mysore, 1936.
2. ***Epigraphia Carnatica***, Vol. VIII, Inscriptions of the Shimoga District, Part II, Mysore, 1904.
3. ***Epigraphia Indica***, Vol. XLI, 1975-76, New Delhi, 1989, PP. 118-124.
4. R.S. Panchamukhi (Ed.), ***Karnataka Inscriptions***, Dharwad, 1941.
5. ***South Indian Inscriptions***, Vol. VII, Mysore, 1986, Vol. IX Part II, Mysore, 1986.
6. William Foster (Ed.), ***English Factories in India 1630-1633***, Oxford, 1910; ***English Factories in India 1637-1641***, Oxford, 1912; ***English Factories in India 1646-1650***, Oxford, 1914; ***English Factories in India 1661-1664***, Oxford, 1923; ***English Factories in India 1665-1667***, Oxford, 1925; ***English Factories in India 1668-1669***, Oxford, 1927.
7. ***Livro do Cartazes***, (Book of Sailing Permits) ***Historical Archives of Goa***, (henceforth ***HAG***) Ms. No.1363.

8. ***Livro do Correspondencia do Kanara 1698-1720***,(Book of Correspondence of Kanara) ***HAG***, Ms. No. 1372; ***Livro do Correspondencia do Kanara 1747-1769, HAG***, Ms. No. 1373.
9. Bragança Periera, ***Archivo Portuguese Oriental*** (Records of Portuguese Asia),(Ten Volumes) Bastora, 1936-40.
10. Manuel de Faria Sousa, ***Asia Portuguesa,*** (Portuguese Asia), Porto, 1945-47.
11. J.F.J. Biker (Ed.), ***Collecçao de Tratados e Concertos de Pazes que ó Estado da India Portuqueza fez com os Reis e Senhores com quem teve relações nas Partes da Asia e Africa Orietnal desde o Principio da Conquista até ao fim do Seculo XVIII,***(in 14 *Tomos*) (Collection of Treaties and Agreements), Lisboa, 1881-1887. (Volumes IV, V and VI furnish details on the treaties between the kings of Kanara and the Portuguese).
12. P.S.S. Pissurlencar(Ed.), ***Agentes da Diplomacia Portuguesa na India*** (Agents of Portuguese Diplomacy in India), Bastora, 1952.
13. *Idem* (Ed.), ***Regimentos das Fortalezas da India***, (Instructions or Ordinances for the Fortresses of India), Bastora, 1951.
14. *Idem* (Ed.), ***Assentos do Conselho do Estado***, (Minutes of the Council of State), (in Five Volumes), Bastora, 1953-57.
15. F.C.Danvers, ***Report of the Portuguese Activities Relating to the East Indies***, Delhi, 1991.
16. ***Journal of Bombay Historical Society***, 1928-1932.
17. S. D. Goitien, ***Letters of Jewish Traders***, Princeton University Press, 1972.
18. S. Muhammad Husayn Nainar (Ed.), ***The Knowledge of India Possessed by Arab Geographers Down To 14th Century A.D. with Special Reference To Southern India***, Madras, 1942.
19. The Arab travellers did not make a distinction between the Kanara coast and the Malabar. Hence they considered Mangalore as a part of Malabar.
20. H.A.R. Gibb (Translated and Selected), ***Ibn Batuta Travels in Asia and Africa 1325-1354***, New Delhi, 1992.
21. *Ibid*, PP. 231-232.
22. *Ibid*, P. 234.
23. Mansel Longworth (Ed.), ***The Book of Duarte Barbosa***, New Delhi, 1989.
24. Armando Cortesao (Ed.), ***The Suma Oriental of Tom Pires***, New Delhi, 1990.

25. Edward Grey (Ed.), ***The Travels of Pietro Della Valle in India, Vol. II***, New Delhi, Reprint, 1991.
26. H.L. Nage Gowda, ***Pravasi Kanda India,*** Vol. II, Mysore, 1966, Vol. III, Mysore, 1969, Vol. IV, 1972, Vol. V, Mysore, 1975, Vol. VI, Mysore, 1977.
27. Alexander Hamilton, ***A New Account of the East Indies***, Madras, 1995.
28. Fawcett (Ed.), ***The Travels of Abbe Carre in India and the Near East 1672 to 1674, Vol. III***, New Delhi, 1990.
29. Arthur Coke Burnell (Ed.), ***The Voyage of John Huyghen Linschoten to the East Indies***, New Delhi, 1988.
30. Ludovico de Varthema, ***Itinerario*** , Lisboa, 1949, Milan, 1956.
31. Presently it is known as Ullala.
32. Francis H. Buchanan, ***Journey From Madras Through the Countries of Mysore, Canara and Malabar,***(in 3 Volumes) ***Vol. III***, Madras, 1807., Reprint 1989.
33. Chandrashekhar (Ed.), ***Gomatesvara Charitre*** (in Kannada), Madras, 1951.
34. R. Shama Shastri (Ed.), ***Linganna Kavi Virachita Keladi Nripa Vijayam***,(in Kannada), Mysore, 1973.
35. Tradition mentions that Parashurama *ksetra* consisted of the western coastal region from Maharashtra to Kerala.
36. See the traditions of South Kanara, namely, *Gramapaddhati* and *Sahyadri Khanda*.
37. Sturrock, *Op. Cit.*, P. 12.
38. *Ibid*, PP. 13-14.
39. M. Govind Pai, 'Tulunadu Poorvasmriti', in Heranje Krishna Bhatta (Ed.), ***Govinda Pai Samshodhana Samputa,*** (in Kannada), Manipal, 1995.
40. *Ibid*, P. 32.
41. K. V. Ramesh, M. J. Sharma (Eds.), ***Tulunadina Shasanagalu*** (in Kannada), Mysore, 1978, P.17.
42. *Ibid*, PP. 33-34.
43. *Nakharadavaru* means people belonging to *Nakhara*, the trade guild.
44. K. V. Ramesh, M.J. Sharma, *Op. Cit*, PP. 38-39.
45. ***Epigraphia Indica,*** Vol. IX, P. 22.
46. P. Gururaja Bhat, ***Studies in Tuluva History and Culture***, *Op. Cit.*, P. xviii.

47. *Ibid*, P. xix.
48. Nagendra Rao, "**The Historical Tradition of South Kanara and the Brahmanical Groups: A Study of *Gramapaddhati* and *Sahyadri Khanda***",

    M. Phil. dissertation, Mangalore University, 1995.
49. *Ibid*, P.22.
50. This was a trade guild active in Barkur and Mudabidre.
51. This was another trade guild of South Kanara.
52. K. V. Ramesh, ***A History of South Kanara***, *Op. Cit.*, P. 288.
53. ***SII***, VII, No. 346.
54. ***SII***, VII, Part II, No. 655
55. B. Jagadish Shetty, *Op. Cit.*, 1992, P. 117.
56. ***ARSIE***, 1931-32, No. 282, SII, VII, No. 324.
57. ***SII,*** VII, Nos. 324 and 390., B. Jagadish Snetty, *Op. Cit.* P. 117.
58. P. Gururaja Bhat, ***Studies in Tuluva History and Culture*, *Op. Cit.,*** P. xix.
59. ***SII***, VII, No.344.
60. B Jagadish Shetty, *Op. Cit.*, P. 67.
61. *Ibid.*
62. *Ibid.*
63. *Gramapaddhati* refers to some of the fallen brahmanas working in fields and gardens. We also know that Kota, Havyak and Karhad brahmans themselves produced the goods with both kin labour as well as extended labour.
64. N. Shyam Bhat, ***South Kanara 1799-1860: A Study in Colonial Administration and Regional Response,*** New Delhi, 1998, PP. 18-19; K.V.Ramesh and M.J. Sharma, ***Tulunadina Arasumanetanagalu Mattu Dharmasa-manvaya,*** (in Kannada), Ujire, 1985, P. 47.

2
Agro-Based Craft Production

The studies conducted on the economic history of peninsular India show that craft production was closely related to agricultural production. This is obvious because Indian economy was dependent on agriculture which was the main occupation of the people. Moreover, agriculture produced the raw materials required for craft production. South Kanara, like North Kanara and many other parts of South India, was known for the availability of facilities for agrarian production. Geographical factors favoured the cultivation of food and commercial crops such as paddy, coconut, sugar-cane, cashew nut, arecanut, pepper and a wide variety of vegetables and fruits. Increased cultivation led to the expansion of the economy. It resulted in advancement of agricultural and industrial production. The techniques of production also underwent changes and improved over the years. There were communities like potters, goldsmiths, blacksmiths, leather workers, metal workers, oil pressers, etc. which carried out artisanal activities. Besides these full time artisans, the agricultural producers also took to craft production, particularly during their off-seasons.

The sources of our study, inscriptions, folk traditions, Portuguese documents, English and Dutch records indicate that South Kanara was a region which mainly produced agrarian products. Studies made on other coastal belts of India such as the Coromandel coast, the Bengal region, the Tamil coast and the Malabar region have proved that there was substantial production of craft goods.[1] In fact, Malabar concentrated on the production of pepper and there was also production of textiles and other craft goods. Different kinds of industries existed in the region. They included oil, pottery, textiles, sugar, jaggery, coir, construction of boats and salt.

Besides, there were many traditional artisanal activities carried out by the carpenter, goldsmith, blacksmith, mason, sculptor, weaver, leather worker and others.

The nature of the economy of South Kanara was influenced by the political structure of the region. During the last centuries of Alupa period and later, different parts of this region were ruled by petty principalities like the Bangas, Chautas, Savantas, Bhairarasas and Ajilas. Below them, there were a large number of subordinates called Ballalas and Heggades who wielded influence in different localities. After 11th century A.D. we find the strengthening of the feudal structure with the decline of the Alupa rulers. The Hoysala and Vijayanagara kings only imposed tributary power over this region. These big kingdoms considered South Kanara as a place which fetched considerable governmental revenue in terms of land tax and an outlet to maintain trade contact with the outside world. In fact it was the latter reason which forced the imperial powers to control the coastal region which consisted of certain very strategically located ports which were significant for economic development of the empire. The Nayakas of Ikkeri took interest in the promotion of trade. The smaller principalities were more concerned about petty gains and they always indulged in groupism and infightings. They were only keen to exact the land revenue and therefore encouraged agricultural production. Trade in agrarian goods also brought them revenue. In addition, the people were willing to invest on land and there was commercialization of agriculture. The economic scenario was that of an expanding agrarian economy. Some of the artisans were landowners and they made donations to the temples. This shows not only their affluence but also the interdependence between agriculture and industry. There are references to the plots of land that were owned by the artisans and cultivated with the help of the peasants. They owned private property known as *muliwarg* in the region and it was hereditary in nature. Sanjay Subrahmanyam[2] has rightly observed that South Kanara was a grain surplus region. Obviously, there existed agro-based craft production.

It is argued that medieval India witnessed the transition from combination of agriculture and industry to the differentiation between agriculture and industry, from artisan serving the village community as a whole to serving a single family which paid the artisan in cash or kind. This system has been described as domestic industry which is "necessary adjunct of the subsistence (natural) economy of the household where the conditions for economic activity are fully or mainly produced in the household..."[3] In the case of South Kanara what we could notice is basically the domestic industry. Here craft production was subservient to agrarian production. Moreover, the interdependence between agriculture and industry continued for a major part of pre-modern history.

Nevertheless, domestic industry was essential to the subsistence economy. K.N. Chaudhuri wrote that industrial production always played an important role in the economy. The evolution of settled agriculture implied an early and fundamental division of labour. This was expressed in a separation of functions between food producers, artisans and the service people. The actual details of methods of production and the nature of specialization varied. They were conditioned by the overall features of the regional economy. Peasant communities were capable of weaving cotton cloth and other textiles within single households. There were skilled industrial workers, carpenters, blacksmiths, and potters who practised part time crop raising alongside their respective hereditary crafts. A full time craftsman could not earn a living from his manual skill alone if the size of the market was strictly limited. If the size of market and cost of transport were important determinants of industrial production, the existence of surplus cultivable land provided the artisans with natural insurance against any sudden unexpected variations in demand. By being a subsistence farmer the rural craftsman made sure that his family would not be deprived of minimum supply of food.[4] Therefore, the domestic industry and the flourishing agriculture were largely co-existing and formed the two basic pillars of the economy of South Kanara. A distinction is made between industries that were strictly localised and those which served wider market and varied population.[5] The industries of South Kanara were more localised in nature. Here we will examine the different aspects of agro-based craft production.

We may mention certain evidences regarding the existence of agro-based production. An inscription of the Alupa king Vijayaditya Maravarma[6] belonging to 9th century A.D. mentions that the tax was collected on the sale of cotton. This suggests that cotton was an important item of trade. An inscription belonging to A.D.1641 from Tirthahalli, mentions silk, arecanut, pepper, cocoanut kernels and wood-laden with bamboo baskets, grain, rice, paddy, ragi, salt, jaggory, oil, ghee and other such articles.[7] A copper plate inscription belonging to A.D.1642 gives certain important details. This was a grant for the Mahattu *math* built near the Araga *pethe* of Bhuvanagiridurga by Durga Timmanna. It mentions the freedom from bullock tax as follows: "in the kingdom which we are ruling above the Ghats, in the *tanes* below Aneyaghata, 10 pack bullocks-except tassels, silk, arecanut, pepper and coco-nut kernels-laden with bamboo baskets, grain, rice, paddy, ragi, salt, jaggery, oil, ghee and such articles, you may from time to time bring, and not selling them outside, store them as a fund for the six *darsana*."[8] Another inscription belonging to A.D.1711 mentions silk, wood and other goods for gain- laden with rice, paddy, ragi, salt, acid, rattan, grain, oil, ghi, pulse, jaggory, fruit, cutch, cocoa-nut kernels, cloths, iron, etc.[9] All these evidences refer to agro-based craft production. Perhaps many of these products were important items of trade

Textiles

We come across reference to Patasalakeri in Barkur. The community of weavers was dominant among the settlers here and the name Patasalakeri denoted the settlement of weavers. The term *patta* or *pata* meant cloth, fine cloth, silk cloth, etc. and *pattasaliga* was a silk weaver.[10] Hence, we may think that the Saligas or weavers produced silk cloth here.

Virabhadra was the chief deity of weavers.[11] In Karkala when there was the ceremony to install the statue of Gomatesvara, the Acharyas were given silk cloth by the king Vira Pandya and we do get reference to cloth shops.[12] The tracts round about Mangalore were industrial centres. Kavuru, Boluru and Irvaduru (Urwa) were centres of cloth manufacture.[13] In Basrur there was one *keri* called *Salera keri* meaning street of weavers. Earlier there existed the settlement of weavers.[14] In the neighbouring district of North Kanara there were the settlement of *Patsalis* or silk weavers who were said to have come from Mysore. Their family goddess was Durga Parameshwari whose shrine could be seen at Haladi near Kundapura in South Kanara. In North Kanara, there were the settlements of Jadas or handloom weavers and Padmasalis.[15] This indicates that weavers of South Kanara and North Kanara had certain relations and they might have migrated from the same place. The Baindur inscription dated Saka 1371 mentions *saleyavaru* which might be a reference to the weavers.[16] A Vijayanagara inscription dated 1431 A.D. mentions Patasaligeri.[17] A study made regarding the taxes on industrial production in the Vijayanagara period demonstrated that tax was imposed on cotton textiles. It is argued by S.A. Bari that during the Vijayanagara period large number of taxes were imposed on the various stages of production. There are references to *hathina sunka, which* meant tax on cotton. We also discern reference to tax on looms.[18] Thus it is suggested by Bari that, "...throughout the Vijayanagara period, and all over Karnataka, the tax on looms was levied..."[19]. This meant that in South Kanara during the Vijayanagara period, tax was imposed on different stages of production of cotton textiles.

Duarte Barbosa gives some information regarding the weavers in the western coast. He states that, "There is another set of gentiles, still lower, whom they call chalien, who are weavers and have no other business except to weave cloths of cotton, and some of silk, which are of little value, and are used by common people."[20] We may compare the word chalien with sale or saleyaru or weavers found in the Kanara coast. Perhaps they catered to the needs of poor people in the villages and towns.

The Bobbarya *paddana*, which belongs to pre-14th century period, gives names of cloth manufacturing centres. King Dharma finished his toilet at the hands of the barber and asked his followers to tell him the remedy for having touched the barber. They advised him to take an oil bath in a tank which was constructed for the purpose; and when he had finished it, his servants asked their royal master from where they could get the silken clothes with which they could wipe off the water from his head. Then the king replied thus: A black silken cloth manufactured at Kavuru, a white silken one made at Boluru, a silken cloth called *sopu kambali*, a silken cloth made at Iravaduru, a silken cloth of which one piece could stretch to three hundred *gavudas* (1 *gavuda*=12 miles), a silken cloth which could be soaked with a tear, and a silken cloth which could be hidden between the nail and finger were required. All the silken clothes were brought and the king dried his head with them.[21] This *paddana* is useful in understanding the social custom, silk manufacturing centres in and around Mangalore and the quality of silk produced in South Kanara. However, the *paddana* is not free from exaggeration, for, the length of a piece of silk cloth is said to be 3,600 miles!.

Kavuru, Boluru and Iravaduru were silk cloth manufacturing centres. They are often mentioned in the *paddanas* as places where silk cloth was manufactured. Boluru has still some families of traditional weavers. The Ballala of Parimale reared the children (Koti and Chennaya), supplied them with food, a *mura* of rice, and a piece of thick *pachade* cloth, and a *mandari*. He also presented them with a white silk cloth from Boluru, a black silk cloth from Kaluru (Kavuru) and a girdle.[22]

Cotton was one of the agrarian products from which the state received some income.[23] This raw material was used for the production of cotton cloth. The Italian traveller Pietro

Della Valle described the Bazar of Ullala where there was the sale of abundant white striped linen cloth, which was made in Olala (Ullal), but coarse, such as the people of the country used.[24] There is reference to the green and dark red finer varieties of cloth which was used in the royal houses.[25] The production of these finer varieties of cloth needed advanced technology which was not available in the region. It was possible that these varieties were imported from outside. The fact that finer varieties of cloth was imported from outside regions is proved by the reference to Chinese silk in the inscriptions. The German traveller Mandel Sella who visited India in 1638 stated that there was import of cotton thread and washers cloth to Mangalore and other ports of Malabar.[26] Francis H. Buchanan wrote that raw silk was exported from this place. Also there was import of cloth, cotton thread and blankets.[27] There was the import of blue cotton cloth from Surat, Cutch and Madras, coarse white cotton cloth from Cutch, Bavanagar, and other places north of Bombay. Raw silk for the use of manufacturers above the ghats was imported from China and Bengal. Buchanan noticed that much of the cloth used in the country was brought from above the ghats partly by the merchants of this place and partly by those of Bangalore and Cuddapa.[28]

Sturrock observed that there was no much weaving carried on in Kanara. The Sales were the most numerous, and they as well as the Devangas were of Telugu origin. The Jadas were the Kanarese. The Devangas were a caste of weavers found in all parts of Madras Presidency. They were divided into two large linguistic sections, the Telugu and Kannada Devangas; the former were usually called Devangas while the latter were known as Jadas. [29] Sales were the class of Telugu weavers. The most important sub-divisions of the caste were Padma Sale and Pattu Sale. Many of them were Lingayats and followed the customs of that sect. The Patvegars were a Kanarese caste of silk weavers. The Bilimaggas were a weaver caste of Tulu origin. They spoke a corrupt dialect of Tulu called Poromba.[30]

Salt

We find reference to the production of salt in the coastal region of South Kanara. There are several place-names of South Kanara which are etymologically connected with production or sale of salt. These are Uppinagadi (shop of salt), Uppuru (place of salt), Uppina Kote (fort of salt), etc. There is reference to the salt producing places like Uppina agara (place where salt is available in plenty) [31] and Uppina kala (well of salt).[32] An inscription from Kundapura dated A.D. 1451 states that a gift of 48 *honnus* (gold), which was the income from the salt pans in Kundapura was made to Joyisa Hariyappa.[33] The Mudukeri inscription belonging to Saka 1407 registers a gift of duties on salt made to the temple of Somanatha at Murukeri by Virupaksha Odeya.[34] In the Vijayanagara period, taxes were levied on the manufacture of salt. Tax was imposed on salt pans known as *uppina kavali.*[35] An inscription belonging to 1486 A.D. refers to salt tax which was granted to a temple.[36] The above references indicate that there was the indigenous production of salt in South Kanara and the state derived income from it. Salt was produced in the coastal regions like Kundapura, Kotesvara, Barkur, Udyavara and Pavanje. The Queen of Ullala imposed and collected tax on salt.[37] According to Buchanan salt was made on this coast by a process similar to that used in Malabar; but the quantity manufactured was very inadequate to the demand of the country. The man who manufactured it got from the Government an advance of five *Pagodas* in cash, and of rice to the same amount. He repaid the money, but not the rice, and paid on an average a tax of 43 *Pagodas;* so that in fact Government got from him 38 *Pagodas* for an ordinary salt-field. Larger and smaller ones paid in proportion. The manufacturer sold his salt as he pleased. It was mixed with a considerable quantity of earthy impurities, but not with more than the common salt of Bengal contained. The common price was one *Pagoda* for 1120 *seers.*[38]

Jaggery and Sugar

There are references to the production of sugar-cane in the inscriptions. It was mostly used in the manufacture of jaggery and sugar. Sugar was imported from the ghat region.[39] One inscription belonging to Saka year 1353 mentions the import of sugar the sale of which was restricted by the trade guilds. According to this inscription there arose conflict between the traders of Murukeri and Chaulikeri regarding the sale of sugar. This record prescribes certain regulations for the sale of sugar brought by local and foreign merchants from above the ghats. It states that merchants of Chaulikeri and Murukeri should collectively weigh and store the stock of sugar and that whatever quantity remained unsold should not be taken to Murukeri but should remain in the storehouse to be sold in times of demand.[40] Sugar was brought from outside and it was sold here by the merchants.[41] Similarly jaggery was also imported.[42] In Karkala there was a shop which sold jaggery.[43] In the Vijayanagara period there is reference to a tax known as *kavalidere.* This tax was imposed on jaggery production or sugarcane mills.[44]

During the Keladi rule there was the export of jaggery from the ports of South Kanara.[45] Buchanan noted that in South Kanara only small quantity of sugar-cane was produced mostly by the Christian populace. Ullala was famous for sugar-cane cultivation and a special variety of jaggery known as Ullala jaggery was manufactured. There were two kinds of canes; the white and black canes (*bili* and *kari kabbu*). The same field was not used for the cultivation of sugar-cane every year; between two crops of sugar-cane, two crops of paddy were raised. Rotation of crops was required for sugar-cane cultivation. A piece of land that sow one *mora* of rice produced 4000 canes. These canes were about six feet long, and sold to the jaggery boilers. Hundred canes were priced anywhere in between 50 Paise and one Rupee. The tax levied on the field cultivated with sugar-cane was the same as that cultivated with paddy. The want of firewood was the greatest obstacle to sugar-cane cultivation, the thrash or expressed stem was not sufficient to boil the juice into jaggery. This operation was performed in earthen pots placed over an open fire. According to Buchanan, the jaggery manufactured in South Kanara was hard, black and of a bad quality. Three *maunds* of jaggery valued one *Pagoda*. [46] Perhaps in South Kanara there was no superior quality of jaggery and sugar manufactured in sufficient quantity and these goods were imported from the upghat regions. Nevertheless, jaggery was exported from South Kanara. This was not just due to the local production but also due to the import of jaggery from outside. Like many other goods jaggery also figured in the entrepot trade.

Oil Production

Production of oil was an important industrial activity that thrived in South Kanara. In the inscriptions there are references to *gana*, the machine used for extraction of oil. The *gana* could be run by hand as well as bullocks. The Kotesvara inscription belonging to A.D.1377 refers to *gana manenne*.[47] An inscription belonging to circa 15th century refers to oil produced from *gana*.[48] The Sankaranarayana inscription dated Saka 1302 records a grant of some land and an oil mill by the Mahapradhana Mallaya-Damnayaka for offerings and lamps to the god Sankaranarayanadeva of Kodagi.[49] In the Vijayanagara period taxes were imposed on oil extraction industry. These taxes were known as *ganada sunke*. This tax was on the machinery used in the process of oil extraction.[50] The ritual of maintaining perpetual lamp (*nanda divige*) in temples necessitated production of large quantity of oil.[51] In all probability, these were produced by the local oil producers.

When there was competition for the production of oil, the state took interest in protecting the local oil producers. In fact, the Keladi king Somashekhara Nayaka insisted that the Portuguese should not establish oil mills in Mangalore and Basrur.[52] The Basrur *kadata* [53] belonging to 1745 A.D. makes a specific reference to the existence of the artisans who produced oil. These ganigas are mentioned as being indebted to the rich merchants of the locality. In this *kadata* there is also reference to the shop owned by the son in law of Ganiga Venkatayya. This indicates that sometimes the producer also was the seller of his produce in the shops at the trade centres. The Bailuru *kadata* refers to *ganada* Appaya as being indebted to an important trading family of the region.[54]

Todakukkinar paddana refers to people who worked in the oil mill. In Koti Chennaya *paddana* there is reference to two kinds of oil mills: *kai gana* (oil mill worked with hand) and *hoi gana* (oil mill worked with bull).[55] Here we find reference to the oil makers as one of the tenants of the land. Todakinara ordered eight tenants of the land, which included the oil makers, to build a *matha* there and they built one.[56] Koti and Chennaya went in search of one Sanku, the oil maker and asked: "Where is Sanku the oil maker? We have given him a *kalase* of oil-seeds. Where is one-fourth of *maund* of oil?.[57]

Sturrock wrote that Ganigas were the oil-pressers of Kanara. The Ganigas were subdivided into three sections. These sections were Hegganigas who yoke two oxen to a stone oil mill; Kiriganigas who made oil in the wooden mills; and Ontiyeddu Ganigas who yoke only one animal to the mill. They were said to have originally come from Mysore. Their guru was the head of the Vyasaraya *math* at Anegundi.[58]

The above details suggest that there existed substantial production of agricultural based craft production. There existed close relations between agricultural production and agro-based craft production. It is suggested that large number of taxes on industrial production in the Vijayanagara period demonstrate that commodities were produced on a much larger scale than in previous period. [59]

Notes and References

1. Vijaya Ramaswamy, ***Textiles and Weavers in Medieval South India***, Delhi, 1985; Surendra Gopal, ***Commerce and Crafts in Gujarat, 16th and 17th Centuries: A Study of the Impact of European Expansion and Pre capitalist Economy***, New Delhi, 1975; S. Jayasheela Stephen, ***The Coromandel Coast and Its Hinterland: Economy, Society and Political System,*** *Op. Cit.*

2. Sanjay Subrahmanyam, 'The Portuguese, the port of Basrur, and the rice trade 1600-50', in *idem,* (Ed.), ***Merchants, Markets and the State in Early Modern India,*** *Op. Cit.*, P. 20.

3. Alexander I Tchitcherov, ***India Changing Economic Structure in the Sixteenth Eighteenth Centuries Outline History of Crafts and Trade***, *Op. Cit.,* P.25. After discussing about the domestic industry he goes to argue that due to gradual feudalisation of the economy there was the creation of the separate class of the artisans who emerged from the peasant community. See PP. 25-28. This argument may be applied in the case of South Kanara also.

4. K.N.Chaudhuri, ***Asia Before Europe: Economy and Civilization of the Indian Ocean from the Rise of Islam to 1750***, *Op. Cit.*, P.298.

5. *Ibid* P.301. Chaudhuri further says that "the distance scale of local production, even when it was not confined to the immediate locality of a particular village, seldom exceeded one day's travel on foot or by slow-moving carts. Production for the inter-regional or trans-continental trade on the other hand involved much longer journeys and called for an elaborate commercial organisation." The craft production in South Kanara was a localised one.

6. ***Epigraphia Indica*** Vol. IX, P.22.

7. ***E.C.,***VIII, Tirthahalli, No. 49.

8. ***Epigraphia Carnatica*** , VIII, Tirthahalli, 42.

9. *Ibid,* Tirthahalli, No. 72.

10. One Mudabidre inscription mentions *chinapatta*, which means silk cloth. ***SII,*** Vol. VII, No. 196.

11. B. Vasantha Shetty, *Op.Cit*, P.276.

12. Y.Umanath Shenoy, ***Karkalada Sri Gomateswara Charitre***, *Op.Cit,* PP.33 and 38.

13. S. Silva, ***Mangalore***, Ankola, 1956, P.16.

14. B. Lakshminarayana Upadhya, 'Pravasigara Tana Basruru Nagara Noda Banni' in, ***Hesarada Pattana Basaruru Ondu Adhyayana*** (in Kannada), Basrur, 1997, P.12.

15. James M. Campbell, ***Gazetteer of the Bombay Presidency Vol., XV, Part I, Kanara***, Bombay, 1883, P.275.

16. K.G.Vasanthamadhava, 'Baindurina Eradu Shilashasanagala Adhyayana', (in Kannada) in ***Itihasa Darshana***, Vol. 14, Bangalore, 1995, PP.144-145.

17. ***SII***, XXVII, No. 102.

18. Syed Abdul Bari, "Non-Agrarian Taxation in Karnataka under Vijayanagara (1336-1565) (A Study in economic transformation based on fiscal systems other than land revenue), op.cit., pp. 35-37.

19. *Ibid*, P. 37.

20. Duarte Barbosa, *A Description of the Coasts of East Africa and Malabar in the Beginning of the Sixteenth Century,* (Translated from an early Spanish Manuscript in the Barcelona Library with Notes and a Preface by Henry E.J. Stanley), New Delhi, 1995, Reprint. (first published London, 1866), P. 136.

21. ***Indian Antiquary*** Vol., XXIII, P.98; B.A. Saletore, *Op. Cit*, P.484.

22. B.A. Saletore, *Op. Cit.*, P.485.

23. K.V.Ramesh, ***A History of South Kanara***, *Op. Cit.*, P.247.

24. Edward Gray, ***The Travels of Pietro Della Valle in India***, Vol. II, *Op.Cit*, P.304.

25. H. L. Nage Gowda, 'Pravasi Kanda Dakshina Kannada' (in Kannada), Adyanadka Krishna Bhatta (Ed.) ***Sudarshana***, Mulki, 1977, P.89.

26. *Ibid*, P.95.

27. Francis H. Buchanan, *Op. Cit*, Volume III, P.4.

28. *Ibid*, PP. 59-60.

29. John Sturrock, *Op. Cit*, P.166.

30. *Ibid*, P. 167.

31. ***SII,*** Vol. VII, Nos. 359, 360, SII, Vol. IX, Part II, No. 409.

32. *Ibid*, No. 295, 261.

33. *Ibid*, Vol. IX Part II, No.455.

34. ***ARSIE***, 1930-31, No. 250.

35. Syed Abdul Bari, *op. cit.,* P. 43.

36. ***SII*** XXVII, No. 151.

37. H. L. Nage Gowda, *Op. Cit.*, P.94.

38. F.H. Buchanan, *Op. Cit.*, PP. 57-58.

39. Shaila Bai U, "**Dakshina Kannada Jilleya Shasanagala Samskritika Adhyayana**", *Op.Cit*, P.233.

40. ***SII***, Vol. VII, No. 309.

41. B. Jagadish Shetty, *Op.Cit*, P.176.

42. ***SII***, Vol. VII, No.340.

43. Y. Umanath Shenoy, *Op.Cit.*, P.38.

44. Syed Abdul Bari, *op. cit.,* PP. 41-42.

45. K.G.Vasanthamadhava, 'Dakshina Kannada Jilleya Itihasa Samikshe', (in Kannada), in Adyanadka Krishna Bhatta, *Op. Cit.*, P. 109.

46. F.H. Buchanan, *Op. Cit.*, PP 43-44.

47. ***SII***, Vol., VII, No.417.

48. ***SII,*** XXVII, No. 400. The exact words used in the inscription are: '*ganadinda nadasuva yellenne taiga...*'

49. ***ARSIE*** 1927-28, No.401.

50. Syed Abdul Bari, *op. cit.,* PP. 39-40.

51. ***SII,*** XXVII, No. 341.

52. J. F. J. Biker, ***Colleccao de Tratados e Concertos de Pazes***, IV, Lisbon, 1884, P.192.

53. Basrur *kadata* in the collections of K. G. Vasanthamadhava, Pavanje.

54. Bailuru *kadata* in the collections of Manjunath Shenoy, Gangolli.

55. B. A. Vivek Rai, *Op. Cit.,* P.203.

56. ***Indian Antiquary***, Vol. XXIII, P.99.

57. *Ibid*, Vol. XXIV, P. 151.

58. John Sturrock, *Op. Cit.*, PP. 167-168.

59. Syed Abdul Bari, *op. cit.,* P. 35.

3

Non-Agro Based Craft Production

Apart from agro-based craft production, there also existed non-agricultural production. Our sources mention the activities of artisans and craftsmen like potters, carpenters, gold smiths, blacksmiths, stone-cutters, etc. The terms artisan and craftsman are closely related to each other. Both indicate use of certain skill possessed by the producers. However, there existed difference as well between the two categories. Perhaps, artisans possessed lesser skill than the craftsmen did. Artisans were involved in large-scale production to cater to the needs of the local people. Thus, there existed both similarities and differences between artisans and craftsmen.

There was increase in the number of craftsmen in South Kanara due to migration of these people into this region. Below we will see the aspects related to migration of craftsmen to South Kanara. Douglas E. Haynes and Tirthankar Roy have discussed about the migration of artisans in India. They argued that some sections among weavers were always mobile, always willing to evacuate from regions in decline and move to those showing signs of expansion. The migration was also due to the encouragement given by the ruling class which wanted increased production of textiles in the capital city. The weavers migrated to those ports where there was greater potential for export of textiles.[1] During the Vijayanagara period, the Devangas migrated from Karnataka and Andhra to the Tamil region due to the expansion of the Vijayanagara empire to the Tamil south.[2] Before the colonial period, the weavers of Andhra, Padmasalis, who produced cotton textiles migrated to Western India.[3] A.I.Tchitcherov has written that the migration of artisans and peasants from their villages was a widespread form of class

Centres of Crafts Production in South Kanaara

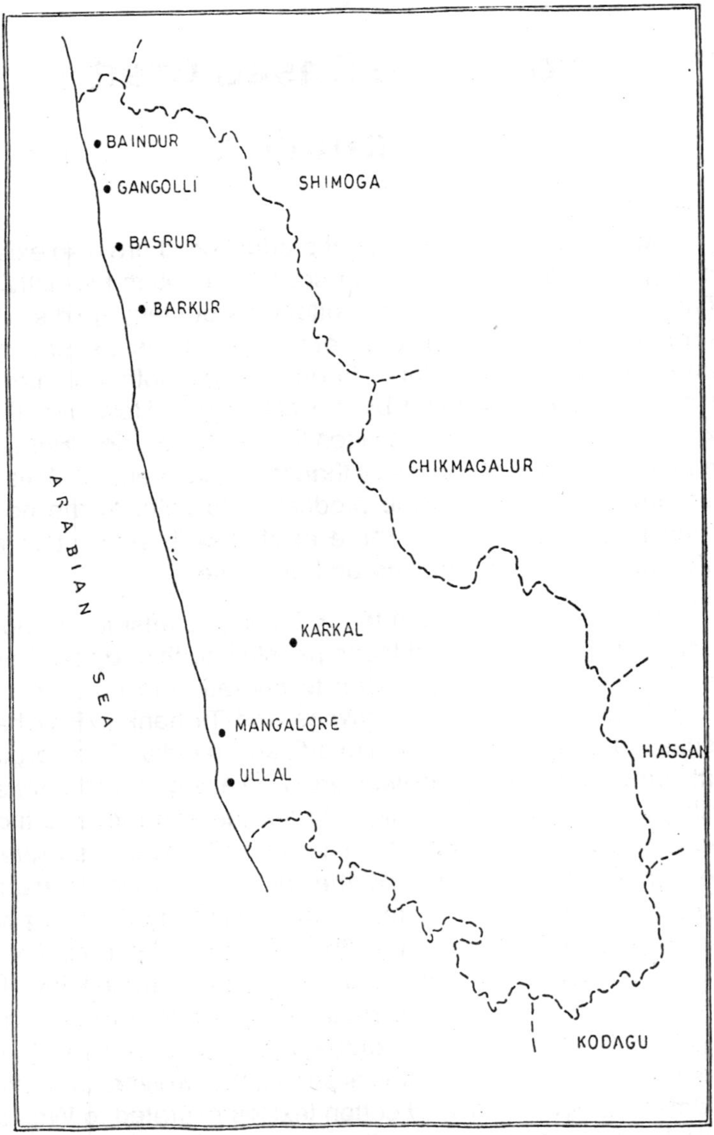

struggle and there was a certain social mobility among the village community artisans.[4] The migration of people might be due to oppressive taxation as mentioned in the Vijayanagara inscription belonging to the period of Achyutadeva Raya.[5] Meera Abraham suggested that the influx of a non-agricultural population into urban areas might have been caused by increased long-distance trade, the development of crafts such as weaving and local trade, all of which would predispose towards the development of urban commercial nuclei.[6]

The hypothesis that artisans and servicemen might have migrated to South Kanara from outside is supported by the sources. The Dharmasthala copper plate inscription reveals interesting details.[7] This inscription belongs to Saka year 1622. It speaks about the conflict between the washermen (*agasaru*) and the musicians (*olagadavaru*) since the latter violated the earlier custom of giving respect to the washermen by using the symbol of white cloth. This matter was taken by the aggrieved party to the court. The matter was decided by a reference to the earlier decision taken at Kanchi. The fact that the controversy was settled by referring to an outside region indicates that the people remembered their earlier connections with that region. The inscription mentions many persons and places which are territories outside South Kanara. If they were indigenous people indeed, there was no need to refer to an outside territory. There is reference to the *gramapramukhas* at the village level. They were Doddachilli Raghava Shettaru and Gramadhipati Guruva Nayaka. Doddadayalapuri Venkatappa argued in favour of the musicians. Venkatappa of Doddapyatepalya argued in favour of the washermen. Fine was paid to *Hagalu* (which means day in Kannada) god of Chennapattana. It was decided to follow the earlier rule as enshrined in the Kanchi charter. The reference to people and persons outside South Kanara clearly indicates that they had migrated, probably from the Tamil region or other parts of Karnataka. In Kashipatnam or Salur (Karkal Taluk), one dateless Telugu inscription in late characters is discovered. It records the obeisance of Suryanarayana, son of Tiruvidhula Venkaya.[8] The name indicates that he belonged to the Telugu region and it is quite possible that he might have migrated to South Kanara and settled there with some occupation.

The medieval period saw the migration of artisans. It also saw the migration of Brahmans on the Western coast.[9] The dynasties like Kadambas established Brahman settlements to strengthen their power in the region. The *agraharas*, the Brahman villages consisted of non-Brahmanical people. They served the Brahmans who did not indulge in any kind of materially productive activities. Thus, it was likely that there was the migration of artisans to South Kanara from other parts of Karnataka and the Peninsula. The ports of South Kanara like Mangalore, Basrur, Gangolli, Baindur, etc. did not attract the settlement of artisans within their borders. Skilled labour generally came into work from outer suburbs.[10] Artisans such as carpenters, stone masons, goldsmiths and others flocked to the ports. All these were taxed on caste basis and the caste heads were used in collecting taxes and paying the state.[11]

Industrial Production

Our sources do not give considerable information on industrial production during the Alupa period. However, during this period, several Shaiva temples were built and also several inscriptions were issued by the Alupa kings. Therefore, we can infer that there was some amount of artisanal activities during this period. The Hoysala period witnessed certain artisanal activities in South Kanara. The inscription of the Hoysala queen Chikkayi Tayi dated 1334 A.D. mentions the construction of the wooden bridge and its maintenance. The grant was given by Chikkayi Tayi for the maintenance of a wooden bridge constructed across the river which touched the western part of Barkur and encircled Bennekudru, a small island to the west of Barkur. The stone poles were installed in the river on which a wooden framework with wooden planks was placed. This bridge connected Barkur with Bennekudru which was well known for sugar-cane and coconut cultivation. Width of the bridge could be about four feet as it was made of three planks. Income from Harady, a part of Brahmavara-west, administered by

Tirimalesvara Nayaka was set apart for the maintenance of this bridge and the responsibility of maintaining this bridge was that of Tirimalesvara Nayaka himself.[12] This shows that there existed a class of carpenters who worked in the public projects initiated by the state.

The inscriptions allude to the existence of artisanal activities. Madivalas or washermen had a separate colony called *Madivalabettu*.[13] There was also the existence of *Bestarabettu* or colony of fishermen. Temples employed a large number of people who performed different functions. Regarding the washermen, Duarte Barbosa states that, "The men are those that wash, and they wash in their houses in large tanks and reservoirs which they have got for this purpose...They wash for a great many people for money, so that they serve all with cleanliness, and they all gain their livelihoods very sufficiently."[14]

Potters employed by the temples were paid through agricultural produce. The Barkur inscription dated 1359 A.D. refers to the payment of five *mudes* of paddy for the potters for one year.[15] The same inscription also refers to the payment through agricultural produce to the carpenters who did the work of the *math*. Pipers or *olagadavaru* formed a separate class of Sappaligas or Seregaras or Devadigas. These artisans and servicemen were employed by the temple.[16] Inscriptional evidences show that grants were given to persons who cleaned the temples. They allude to *Maletharu*, that is, land granted to the people who supplied male or garland for the worship of God in temples.[17] The potters had to supply *panate* or *hanate* (earthen lamp) and their work is mentioned as *kumbaragarike*.[18] The Tulu proverbs refer to oil maker, goldsmith, potter, leather worker, blacksmith, weaver (*Jedarava*)[19] and their activities in the society of South Kanara.

Another record dated 1377 A.D. refers to the payment to the ladies who rendered services to the temple. It mentions that two persons who did *chamaraseve* were paid two *nadahanes* daily. It mentions that Basavetti was paid two *mudes* and two *hanes* for the whole year.[20] The Kukke Subrahmanya inscription belonging to Saka year 1309 mentions that potters Mudiya Setti and Belli Setti were the joint donees of land grant which consisted of the bowers and betel-nut, mango, jack and pepper groves and the tax amount of four *nishkas.* [21] This land grant would have certainly made these potters affluent in the society. An inscription belonging to Udupi Taluk dated Saka year 1323 refers to Virachari's son Nambiyachari.[22] During the Vijayanagara period, we find reference to *kumbaradere* which was a tax imposed on potters.[23]

Although the profession of the achari (an artisan working in metal or wood) is not mentioned here, we may presume that artisanal occupation had become hereditary and was pursued by particular castes. We find references to artisans owning land. There is reference to the garden of achari.[24] This is not surprising because there existed the practice of remunerating the temple servants through assignments of land. Besides as noted earlier, many of the land owners also took to craft production. An epigraph of 1402 A.D. mentions *badagiya bayalu* (carpenter's field) which reveals ownership of paddy fields by the carpenters.[25] This inscription also mentions *kumbaradi*, a place inhabited by kumbaras or potters. An epigraph belonging to A.D.1546 mentions the field owned by potter.[26] It is possible that artisans had established their own *mathas*. One inscription belonging to A.D.1562 mentions *akkasaleya mathada gadi.*[27] It seems to be a usual practice to build *maths* by rich communities. An inscription belonging to A.D.1608 mentions the property of potters (*kumbara hakala vivara*).[28] The artisans owned both kinds of lands, wet and dry. The bettu lands indicate the dry character of the land owned by the artisans.[29] However there are references to wet lands owned by artisans. There is reference to *badagiya bayala gadde* and *accukottariya gadde.*[30] The remuneration of the artisans was paid both in kind and cash. The Uppunda inscription dated Saka 1369 registers gift of land for providing *Panchavadya* during the *Sribali* service in the temple.[31] Another inscription dated Saka 1405 registers gift of land for the maintenance of the Piper who played during the *Sribali* service in the temple.[32] This practice of giving land grants to the artisans and other servicemen prevailed in other parts of South India also. In fact, in South India during the Vijayanagara period most of the villages consisted of the artisans and servicemen who were given land grants. The remuneration in kind was called *ayam* or *aya* and craftsmen were known as *ayagars*.[33]

There is reference to the artisans like potter, blacksmith, goldsmith, carpenter, shoemaker and others. They were attached to the villages. A share of the peasant production was given to them.[34] Duarte Barbosa mentions the section of people who were potters and workers of clay called 'Cujaven'. He states that, "Their business is to work at baked clay, and tiles for covering houses, with which the temples and Royal buildings are roofed; and by law no other persons may roof their houses except with palm branches."[35] While it is difficult to identify Cujaven in context of South Kanara, we can infer that it referred to the potters community in the society of South Kanara. The Kukke Subrahmanya temple inscription belonging to A.D. 1665 refers to a land grant which was donated by gold smiths who originally belonged to Gujarat.[36] There are evidences to suggest that there existed certain settlements of people from Gujarat. For instance in an inscription belonging to A.D. 1542 mentions community called 'Gujaras' in a place called Bennekuduru.[37] The above references belong to 16th and 17th centuries. Hence migration and settlement of Gujaratis must have begun after this period. Earlier we have mentioned that there was migration of artisans into South Kanara.

An inscription belonging to 1570 A.D. refers to the house of a potter.[38] The Kollur temple inscription belonging to A.D. 1708 mentions that tax was imposed and collected from potters.[39] The Koti Chennaya *paddana* mentions the potters (odari or kumbara) [40] Koti and Chennaya went to one Abbu, the potter and asked: "We have given you a *kalase* of paddy, where are small and large earthen vessels?"[41] The Bailuru *kadata* mentions that Kumbara Chikku borrowed a loan from the rich merchant of the region.[42] This indicates that some of the merchants of the region had already emerged as moneylenders. The poorer artisans and farmers would have borrowed loans from them.

The carpenters, stone cutters and sculptors were in great demand. In the preparation of huge wooden cars (chariots) and wooden images of gods and goddesses carpenters exhibited their skill besides doing their part of the work in building temples and other structures. The wooden chain and the bead in the Panchalingesvara temple and the wooden images in the Mahishasura temple at Mudukeri, Barkur, are some of the examples of their craftsmanship. Huge wooden figures called *tattirayas*, used for procession, also provided the opportunity for the carpenters to exhibit their skill.[43] The work of Duarte Barbosa refers to carpenters. He states, "Another lower lineage amongst these gentiles is called ajare. Their business is that of quarrymen and carpenters, and others are blacksmiths, carvers of metals, and silversmiths."[44] Obviously here, the word 'ajare' refers to 'achari' used in South Kanara to carpenters and other artisans and craftsmen. An inscription belonging to 14th century A.D. refers to *kammara salu*.[45] It may indicate either the existence of workshop of blacksmiths or that it may refer to streets of blacksmiths. In any case, this would lead to the conclusion that there was large-scale production of commodities which made the villages self sufficient as far as the supply of iron implements are concerned. Blacksmiths became very important part of an agrarian economy as they were approached by agriculturists for manufacture and repair of agricultural implements. An inscription belonging to A.D. 1542 refers to agrarian activities of a blacksmith. In this context the word used to mean blacksmith is *kammara*.[46] The use of the term *kammara kodage* in an inscription belonging to 1449 A.D.[47] may indicate that irrigation works were constructed and maintained by blacksmiths and other artisan communities. The fact that blacksmiths played an important role in land transactions has been highlighted in an inscription belonging to A.D. 1725.[48]

Copper brought from outside was used in Barkur for preparation of vessels and taken inland for coinage.[49] In South Kanara, during the Vijayanagara period and also during the

Keladi period, there existed two minting places, at Mangalore and Barkur.[50] It is possible that artisans were employed by the state to produce the coins. The main duty of the officer of mint house was to maintain the purity and weight of coins that were produced in his mint. This was done with the help of the goldsmiths who were appointed by the government. This means that they were the government servants and not private artisans.[51] This was another means of introducing alien artisans into South Kanara. These artisans always used to carry with them necessary instruments to check the purity and weight of the coins. They were very shrewd and had mastered their profession.[52] Even a petty principality like that of the Bangas had its own *gadyanas*.[53] The copper plate inscriptions refer to wood work and copper work in Karkala.[54] An inscription mentions that taxes were granted to the temple in Kota for the maintenance of a hand-lamp in the temple.[55] It is possible that the hand-lamp were produced within the locality itself.

There are not many inscriptions mentioning *kallukuttigas* (stone cutters or sculptors). Nevertheless, we cannot undermine their importance. The stone inscriptions, beautiful sculptures and temples suggest the role that they played in South Kanara. Besides doing their work as sculptors, they engraved inscriptions and thus helped the rulers to publicise their orders and commemorate their munificent deeds.[56] The Kallukuttiga *paddana*[57] mentions about the activities of the stone workers. It mentions the construction of Jain monuments in Karkala.[58] The existence of Brahman and Jain settlements must have facilitated the craftsmanship of the stone workers because there was the need for the construction of temples and *basadis*. The artisans are referred to as Acchava in *Kallurti paddana*. The artisans are also known as Vishwakarma Brahmans and Panchalas. The *Kallurti paddana* mentions Kanchidesa.[59] This must be a reference to Kanchi of Tamil Nadu which was an important trade and craft centre during the historical times. There is a tradition that artisans migrated from Kanchi to Vijayanagara. The Vishwakarmas of Karnataka even today send their contributions to Kanchi. Those who collected these contributions are called *Ponos Makkalu*, who follow the traditional occupation of collecting money to be given to Kanchi.[60] The *paddana* also mentions Aigundi *samsthana* which is actually a reference to the *math* of Vishwakarmas of Anegundi.[61] When South Kanara became a part of Vijayanagara empire, artisans migrated from Andhra and other parts of the Kannada region. All the artisans did not migrate to South Kanara at the same time. Looking at the architecture of the region, it can be held that stone workers came here during the 7th-8th century A.D. Later during the rule of Cholas, bronze workers might have come during the 10th century. During the period of Hoysalas stone workers came from Belur and Hasana. During the Vijayanagara rule many artisans came from Hampi. Other artisans, for example, carpenters and blacksmiths migrated from Kerala and Shimoga. The *paddanas* refer to *tacchavaru* from Malenadu. Earlier there existed the non-aryan blacksmiths who produced iron goods. The *paddanas* refer to them as *karbotigare* or *kadtalegare*. Later there was the migration of aryan bronze workers who were called *kanchugaras* and they migrated from Kanchi. There was the migration of gold workers from North Karnataka.[62] In the Kalikamba temple at Barkur there is a figure of camel. Since camel was a rare animal in South Kanara it is possible that this was the work of an artisan from North India.[63] In South Kanara there exists a community of artisans who are goldsmiths called Daivajna Brahmans. They are supposed to have migrated from North India.[64] The attempt to call themselves Brahmans indicate the influence of the brahmanical ideology on them and also their interest to occupy an important position in the ritual hierarchy in the graded brahmanical society. Some of the artisans were called acharya or achari, which means they were master craftsmen and they had a few apprentices. Kenneth R.Hall suggests that this distinction between *acharya* and "superintending" artisans on the one hand and labouring artisans on the other may also be seen as a reaction to the extension of Brahmanical ideology.[65]

The busy trade and commerce on the Kanara coast facilitated the growth of a number of main and allied industries. The existence of several *keris* (streets) at Barkur, Basrur,

Karkala and Mudabidre represented possibly the various industries run by different guilds and the settlements of artisans. Many of these industries must have been run by rich Jain merchants and guilds, employing skilled labourers irrespective of religion or caste.[66]

Notes and References

1. Douglas E.Haynes and Tirthankar Roy, 'Conceiving mobility: Weaver's migrations in pre-colonial and colonial India' ***Indian Economic and Social History Review*** (henceforth *IESHR*), XXXVI, Number 1, Jan-March 1999. P.36.

2. *Ibid,* P.43.

3. *Ibid*, P.55.

4. Alexander I. Tchitcherov, *Op.Cit*, P.39.

5. ***Annual Report of South Indian Epigraphy*** (henceforth ***ARSIE***), 1916, No.69.

6. Meera Abraham, ***Two Medieval Merchant Guilds of South India***, *Op. Cit.,* P.117.

7. Keladi Gunda Jois, "Dharmasthaladalliruva Tamrashasana" (in Kannada), ***Lochana*** (Publication details are not available).

8. ***ARSIE***, 1953-54, No.340.

9. See Kesavan Veluthat, ***Brahman Settlements in Kerala: Historical Studies***, Calicut, 1978; Nagendra Rao, "**The Historical Tradition of South Kanara and the Brahmanical Groups: A Study of *Gramapaddhati* and *Sahyadrikhanda***", *Op. Cit*, 1995, P. 22.

10. S.Arasaratnam, ***Maritime India in the Seventeenth Century***, *Op. Cit.*, P.16.

11. *Ibid*, P.225.

12. B.Vasantha Shetty, "**Barakuru- A Metropolitan City of Antiquity**", *Op.Cit.*, 1985, PP.137-139.

13. ***ARSIE*** , 1931-32, No.282.

14. Duarte Barbosa, *A Description of the Coasts of East Africa and Malabar in the Beginning of the Sixteenth*

Century, (Translated from an early Spanish Manuscript in the Barcelona Library with Notes and a Preface by Henry E.J. Stanley), New Delhi, 1995, Reprint. (first published London, 1866), p. 135. (henceforth, *A Description of the Coasts*) pp. 135-136.

15. ***SII,*** Vol.VII, No.334.

16. B.Vasantha Shetty, *Op.Cit.*, P.401; B.Jagadish Shetty, "**Agro-Economic Relations and Social Structure in Dakshina Kannada (A.D.1000-1600)**", *Op. Cit.*, PP. 182-183.

17. ***SII*** Vol. VII, No.377.

18. *Ibid,* No.330.

19. B.A.Vivek Rai, ***Tulu Janapada Sahitya*** (in Kannada), Bangalore, 1985, PP.475-478.

20. ***SII***, Vol. IX Part II, No.417.

21. K.V.Ramesh, 'No.13- Kukke (Subrahmanya) Grant of Madhavaraja, Kali 4488 and Saka year 1309'***Epigraphia Indica***, Vol. XLI, 1975-76, P.121.

22. ***SII***, Vol. VII, No.267.

23. Syed Abdul Bari, *op. cit.,* P. 73.

24. ***SII,*** Vol. VII, No.342.

25. *Ibid,* No.324.

26. ***SII***, Vol. IX Part II, No. 620.

27. *Ibid*, No.673.

28. *Ibid*, No.694.

29. B.Jagadish Shetty, *Op.Cit.*, P.117.

30. ***SII*** Vol. VII, Nos.324 and 390.

31. ***ARSIE*** 1929-30, No. 553.

32. *Ibid*, No.552.

33. Burton Stein, *The New Cambridge History of India Vijayanagara,* Cambridge, 1989, P. 7.

34. Alexander I. Tchitcherov, *Op.Cit,* P. 46.

35. Duarte Barbosa, *A Description of the Coasts*, p. 135.

36. K.G. Vasanthamadhava, *Karavali Karnataka Samskritika Itihasada Aakaragalu Bhaga I, Puratatva Shastradharagalu,*(in Kannada), Unpublished manuscript, p. 319; *Mysore Archaeological Report 1943,* No. 49.

37. ***SII,*** XXVII, No. 185.

38. *Ibid*, No. 199.

39. K.G. Vasanthamadhava, *Karavali Karnataka Samskritika Itihasada Aakaragalu Bhaga I, Puratatva Shastradharagalu*, p. 336.

40. B. A. Vivek Rai, ***Tulu Janapada Sahitya***, *Op.Cit.,* P. 178.

41. ***Indian Antiquary***, Vol. XXIV P. 151.

42. Unpublished *kadata* (undated) which I found in the house of Manjunath Shenoy, Gangolli. This *kadata* may be dated to late 18th century.

43. B.Vasanth Shetty, *Op.Cit*, P. 402.

44. Duarte Barbosa, *A Description of the Coasts,* p. 140.

45. ***SII,*** XXVII, No. 341.

46. *Ibid*, No. 185.

47. ***SII,*** XXVII, No. 362.

48. K.G. Vasanthamadhava, *Karavali Karnataka Samskritika Itihasada Aakaragalu,* p. 340.

49. *Ibid*, P. 314.

50. There is reference to '*Barakura gadyana*' in ***SII***, Vol. VII, Nos.223, 231. '*Mangulura gadyana'* is referred in the same volume, Nos. 189,223.

51. A.V.Narasimha Murthy, ***Vijayanagarada Nanya Sampattu*** (in Kannada), Mysore, 1996, P. 20.

52. *Ibid,* P. 20 and P. 52.

53. Y.Umanath Shenoy, ***Karkalada Sri Gomatesvara Charitre*** (in Kannada), Ujire, 1991, P. 38.

54. Ho.Na.Nilakantha Gowda and M.G.Manjunatha, 'Mudabidare Jaina Mathada Aprakatita Tamra Shasanagalu'(in Kannada), ***Itihasa Darshana***, Vol.14, Bangalore, 1995, P. 62.

55 ***SII,*** XXVII, No. 243.

56 B.Vasanth Shetty, ***Op.Cit.***, P.403.

57 Paltadi Ramakrishna Achar, ***Kalkuda Kallurti Samskriti Shodha*** (in Kannada), Puttur, 1998, PP.17-25.

58 For details on Jainism in South Kanara, see, P. N. Narasimha Murthy, *Op. Cit*; K.G.Vasantha Madhava, ***Religions in Coastal Karnataka 1500-1763,*** *Op. Cit*.

59 Paltadi Ramakrishna Achar, *Op.Cit,* P.49.

60 *Ibid*, P.51.

61 *Ibid*, P.52.

62 *Ibid*, PP. 55-56.

63 *Ibid*, P.68.

64 *Ibid*, P.66.

65 Kenneth R. Hall, ***Trade and Statecraft in the Age of Cholas***, New Delhi, 1980, P.107.

66 P.N.Narasimha Murthy, *Op.Cit,* P.475.

4

Trade, State and Society

The economy of South Kanara was predominantly agricultural and craft production was its another pillar. It was because of the agrarian surplus that trade started in the agrarian goods like rice and pepper. Different parts of Indian subcontinent specialised in the production of different commodities - both agrarian as well as non-agrarian. Trade emerged with the exchange of these goods. In the context of the Chola state, K. R. Hall argued that even in an agrarian society trade seemed to arise naturally as a result of geographic dispersal of the products of the soil, due to their different requirements of temperature, humidity, soil quality, etc. Only certain areas of Indian subcontinent produced spices, pepper and this necessitated trade to articulate their distribution to non-producing areas. Similarly arecanuts and betel leaves, items seemingly used throughout the subcontinent even in early times were products of a palm tree that required a specific habitat. Thus, according to Hall, although ancient Indian society was essentially agrarian, historical sources present evidence that within this society trade flourished.[1] The arguments of Hall are applicable to the context of South Kanara during the period under study.

In the inscriptions we find reference to the Settis who are mentioned as landlords. Settis also formed one of the important categories of traders in the region. Thus some of the traders emerged from the class of landlords. In ancient India there was the emergence of *grahapati* traders who were actually the householders or the owners of land.[2] The surplus production in agrarian goods facilitated these people to involve in trade. Naturally there was interaction with the outside region.

There was the migration of traders from neighbouring regions to South Kanara and they were called *horahinavaru* (outsiders). Some of the traders belonged to the Brahmanical religion and some others belonged to Jainism. They gave donations to the temple in terms of land grants and money donations. Gradually there was a need for the establishment of systematic rules and regulations to facilitate smooth trade of the goods and also to protect their own interests. The traders formed trade guilds which protected their interests and also decided cases of conflict between them.

During this period South Kanara was ruled by Alupa, Hoysala, Vijayanagara and Keladi rulers. The rulers realised the importance of encouraging traders because trade brought considerable revenue to the Government. They also encouraged agriculture which fetched land revenue to the state and agriculture provided the basis for trade in South Kanara. Both kings and traders were responsible for the establishment of urban centres. These urban centres emerged because of politico-administrative factors like headquarters of the rulers, economic factors like trade and religious factors. The kings also encouraged the construction of number of temples and they granted lands to these temples. By this they tried to establish their authority in their territories.

In South Kanara there was the emergence of important urban centres like Mangalore, Buntwal, Barkur, Basrur, Karkala, Mudabidre, Venur, Baindoor, Gangolli, etc. Some of these centres like Mangalore, Buntwal, Barkur, Basrur, Baindoor and Gangolli were coastal towns, while the centres like Karkal, Mudabidre and Venur were interior towns and were well-known for the existence of Jainism. In all these centres we find the Hindu temples.

Tolls, Customs and Transit Duties

There existed trade transactions between the ghat regions and the low lying plains on the Western coast. The state collected tolls in the strategic places where the goods arrived. The tolls formed an important source of revenue for the state. An inscription of the Alupa king Vijayaditya Maravarma[3] belonging to 9th century A.D. mentions that the king confirmed the tolls due to the city of Pombuccha together with the city of Udayapura. The goods were taxed in the following manner:

Item	*Tax*
2 bags of grain	1½ baskets of grain
1 *malave* of cotton	16 *pala* of cotton
1 load of areca nuts	300 nuts
1 load of pepper	16 *pala* of pepper.

Another Alupa inscription of Vijayaditya belonging to 9th century A.D. mentions that the king confirmed the gift of one half of the tolls to the city of Pombuccha together with the city of Udayapura.[4]

The state also imposed taxes on shops. An inscription belonging to A.D. 1536 from Koteswara refers to sales or commercial tax collected from shops (*angadi* in Kannada means shop) amounting to one hundred and thirty six *gadyanas* and twenty *panams.*[5] The studies made in this field revealed that there were taxes on temporary stalls erected in the markets known as *adikasu*. There are also references to sales tax levied on branded cattle. There were taxes on the sale of fish, and on the sale of sheep, horse and bullocks.[6]

The state collected taxes on goods in transit, which entered the cities and towns by both road and waterways. There was also a custom duty levied on the transactions of goods within the state as well as on goods exported from and imported into the state. The volume of trade facilitated the state to impose maximum taxes on trade and traders and extract as much amount as it liked. The tolls collected on the entry of the goods into a region and at the gates of cities varied from place to place. The rate of taxation depended upon the inflow and outflow of goods. The quantum of goods traded determined both the amount of revenue collected and the nature and extent of the trade with which it was linked.

Here one has to make a distinction between the situation

before the emergence of Vijayanagara empire and the scenario after the establishment of Vijayanagara empire. It was the establishment of Vijayanagara empire which gave a great boost to the trade since the state took active interest in protecting the interests of traders. The unification of empire under one uniform system made the transit of goods from place to place more easier.

During the Vijayanagara period, the petty coastal principalities were allowed to extract land revenue while the empire concentrated on collection of the customs of ports and tolls on the highways connecting the ports to imperial city of Vijayanagara. Even in these, the imperial interest was limited to ensuring that the commercial links to the seaboard were not harmed.[7]

The sources refer to two types of custom duties: (i) on the movement of goods from one region to the other within the Vijayanagara state, and (ii) on goods which were either exported from or imported into the Vijayanagara state.[8] There were two important methods of collection of transit and custom duties. One method was leasing out the work of collecting the custom duties, and the other was of the state collecting the dues directly through a network of officials.[9] The Basrur inscription belonging to A.D. 1465 refers to *senabhova* attending the ports to collect the taxes from loaded ships leaving the port of Basrur.[10]

The Karkala inscription dated Saka year 1256 mentions the tax collected on items like salt, pepper, ginger, paddy, rice, etc.[11] The copper plate inscription of Tolara belonging to Saka 1358 registers gift of certain tolls made by Mahapradhana Annappa Odeya to Tolahara Sankara Nayaka, who was administering Yelare, in return for which the latter was to build a *math* attached to the temple of Hattara Narayanadeva at Barkur and feed therein six Brahmans.[12] An inscription dated A.D. 1444 mentions that the *Nakharas* and Settis of Dharmapattana agreed to pay to the temple of Mahadeva a portion of toll-revenue raised in the village.[13] A copy of the inscription dated Saka year 1371 mentions that 240 *katigadyanas* was collected as custom duty at Yanavali river region in Mangalore *rajya*.[14]

An inscription belonging to A.D. 1606 mentions that due to the order of Venkatappa Nayaka all the Mahanad Settis who loaded goods by both roads to places east and north and to the interior gave a *sasana* granting for the Siva services of the *math* one *visa* on the stock as follows: "throughout the kingdom ruled by Venkatappa Nayaka above the Ghats, on all local roads, for all animals, at the rate of one *visa* for each animal, we agree to give as *dharma*, *visa* by *visa,* in all the *thanas.*"[15] The inscription specifies the following *thanas*: Ikkeri, Sagara, Kumbhasi, Pombucha, Agumbe, Bidirur, Belare, Kalasa and Kiga, etc.[16]

The Sirur copper plate inscription belonging to A.D. 1610 gives certain interesting details. The inscription states that Keladi Venkatappa Nayaka conferred on Keriya Sankanna Senabhova alias Narana the office of *sthalasenabhovike*. He was authorised to collect custom duties on agrarian products coming from five *simes*, namely, Ulanadu, Hemmaranadu, Bidaranadu, Baiduru and Haligere. The inscription mentions the existence of *sunkathanes* in these five *simes.*[17] A copper plate inscription belonging to A.D.1642 also gives details regarding the custom duties. This was a grant for the Mahattu *math* built near the Araga *pethe* of Bhuvanagiridurga by Durga Timmanna. It mentions the freedom from bullock tax as follows: "in the kingdom which we are ruling above the Ghats, in the *tanes* below Aneyaghata, 10 pack bullocks-except tassels, silk, arecanut, pepper and coco-nut kernels-laden with bamboo baskets, grain, rice, paddy, ragi, salt, jaggery, oil, ghee and such articles, you may from time to time bring, and not selling them outside, store them as a fund for the six *darsana.*"[18]

The Siddhapur copper plate inscription belonging to Saka 1692 records a gift of customs duties on all articles of merchandise passing through the *nadu.* This gift was made by the Chief, the *Mahanadu, Settis,* etc.[19] An inscription belonging to Saka 1698 mentions the existence of *sunkathane* at Kanjodu, Sullia.[20]

The Halasnadu *kadata* dated A.D. 1752 refers to

sunkathanes at Haladi, Kerladi, Bidruru, Kolluru, etc.[21] The Sringeri *kadatas* mention some of the places where there was the collection of custom duties. They mention Hosangadi, Narasipura, Someshwara, Karkala, Mudabidre, Subrahmanya, Kumble, Manjeshwara, Ullala, Kodeyala (Mangalore), Panamburu, Mulike, Hejemadi, Kapu, Kattupadi, Kalyanapura, Barkur, Savada, Gulvadi, Basrur, Talamaru, Hemmadi, Nayakanakatte, Bayiruru, Bhatkal, Sirali, Honnavar, Gerasope, Chandavara, Midaje, Maruru, Kolluru, etc.[22]

The above details indicate that the transit and custom duties were important sources of revenue for the state. Some of the prominent merchants and trade guilds were also involved in the collection of custom duties. Sometimes the kings and merchants granted a part of the tax to the temples which served the purpose of obtaining religious glory. The traders did not try to avoid the tax when they knew that the tax collected would go to serve the religious purpose.

Pietro Della Valle, the Italian traveller who visited South Kanara noted details about tolls. He stated that, "Having passed by Banghel we entered into the greater Northern River, in which on the left hand is a place where passage-boats laden with Merchandize pay a Toll to the Ministers of Venkatapa Naieka, to whom the circumjacent Region is subject".[23] It seems that the Keladi rulers had appointed certain officials who were in charge of collection of tolls.

The fact that taxes were collected in certain places is also indicated by the study of place names and the traditions related to certain places. There are place names like *Sunkadakatte* and *Ukkudada Katte*. There is reference in the tradition about *Buntwala sunka.*[24]

The Koti Chennaya *paddana* mentions about the toll gate.[25] It informs us that Dere, the toll-taker, saw Koti and Chennaya from a distance, and came down from his verandah and ran away, but they waited for Dere till his return. They saw him coming from a distance, and started onwards and said: "Who is that going along? Is he a Sanbhog? A son of a Jaina

Setti? Is he a Baraga, the son of a Bant?"

"No matter who you are, you must pay the daily toll at Banga's verandah", said Dere.

"Why do you ask toll, Dere ? Have we loads on our heads, Dere? ..." asked they.

"The toll is for your dagger of steel, which you have on", said Dere.

Thus the local Chieftains had appointed officials to collect custom dues. The officer in charge of collection of tax as far as possible tried to extract dues from all sections in the society.

South Kanara had fertile agrarian fields which facilitated increased production of crops. This surplus production led to the growth of trade in agrarian products. South Kanara was known for the production of agrarian commodities like rice, coconut, areca nut, cashew nut, pepper and other crops. Industrial or craft products like sugar, jaggery, wooden and metal tools, cloth, coir, salt, oil, etc. were produced. Some of the craft products, particularly cloth was imported from places like Surat, Bombay and Cuddapah and up ghat regions of Karnataka. The agrarian products may be classified into food products and commercial products. Different varieties of rice, ragi, jowar, vegetables and fruits came under the first category. Sugar-cane, coconut, areca nut, cashew nut, pepper, cardamom and forest products belonged to the second category.[26]

In South Kanara rice was an important food product. But due to the surplus production and the volume of its trade, it became a commercial product. According to Duarte Barbosa, the varieties of rice that were grown in this region were *Girasal, Acal, Quavages* and *Pachary.* White rice was consumed by rich classes and red and black by the poor classes.[27] However we know that in Malabar and Kanara coast red and black rice was consumed both by rich and poor classes. In the Kanara coast white rice was mostly consumed by the brahmans. Thus nature of rice consumption went not through class lines but through caste lines.

There was a growing interest among the rulers to promote agriculture and to increase the production of agrarian commodities. For, they knew that it would bring more revenue to the Government from the agricultural sector. They realised that surplus agricultural products facilitated trade and trade in turn brought revenue to the state. The Nayaks of Keladi encouraged coconut cultivation whenever rice crops failed. A copper plate dated A.D. 1681 from the village Kodladi states that the rice cultivated lands in the places of Padukone and Gangolli incurred *nashta* (loss) and to overcome the loss, the ruler of Keladi, Chennammaji encouraged the cultivation of coconut on the grazy sandy lands and on the sea shore in these places.[28] It is important to note that these coastal areas were best suited for coconut cultivation. Similarly other agrarian products like sugar-cane, ginger, chilli, banana and cashew nuts were cultivated and forest products like medicinal plants, cardamom, cinnamom, etc. were available on both sides of Sahyadri. These products brought considerable income to the state.[29] The copper plate inscription of Rani Shankaradevi Ajila belonging to A.D.1720 mentions the cultivation of arecanut. Arecanut was a conspicuous cash crop of South Kanara during this period. In order to get more income from agriculture the state constructed canals and thereby provided irrigational facilities. Increased cultivation of agrarian products helped the state to obtain more tax.[30]

Traders and Trade Network

The traders participated in both inland and sea trade. This led to contact with outside regions. Inscriptions in other districts of Karnataka mention about the traders of South Kanara. An inscription belonging to A.D.1412 (belonging to Sorab) mentions the lord of ships (*navigada prabhu*), Mangaluru Naga Gauda's son Setti Gauda.[31] This indicates the trade contact between the coastal region and an inland town above the ghats. Besides it also bears testimony to the coastal and overseas trade during the period, for Setti Gauda is referred to as lord of ships and ships were required only for sea trade.

A Hoysala inscription gives interesting detail about the

existence of traders of South Kanara in other regions. The inscription belonging to A.D.1278 while mentioning about the various imposts paid to the Turukas mentions that Tulu-Maleyalas pay 32 *ga* and 5 *pa.*[32] The Mudubidre inscription of Devaraya II (dateless) alludes to the grant of one *kolaga* of paddy on every bullock load coming into the town of Basrur.[33]

A Vijayanagara inscription discovered in Belur and dated Saka year 1304 is of great interest to us. The significance of the inscription lies in the fact that it mentions the varieties of goods that were found in the trade of South Kanara and also there is reference to the different trade guilds of Karnataka and the relations between these trade guilds. The relevant part of the inscription runs thus:

"Rejoicing in the protection of Harihara the farmers and the merchants resolved to pay him certain taxes. In the Saka year 1304 the five hundred *virasasanas* of the Jambudvipa, situated on the southern direction of the Bharatakhanda in the world...;protectors of the righteous customs of the *salumule-bananju* sect; the birth place of *ubhayananadesis* of the celebrated capitals of emperors and kings; the fan-palm of their warehouse (*sitalamalige*); worshippers of the divine and illustrious lotus feet of the gods Ganesvara and Gavaresvara; all the *halavu*, the *nakhara-parivara, mummuri-danda,* all the receivers of dues and the 300 Billa dependants of their guard (*kalgahu*), together with *holiyajanguli* of Vijayanagari, Hastinavati, Dorasamudra, Gutti, Penugundi, Adavani, Udayagiri, Chandragiri, Muluvayi, Kachi, Padevidu, Chadurangapattana, Mangaluru, Barakuru, Honnovura, Chandhavura, Araga, Chandragutti, Annigere, Huligere, Nidugallu, Chimatanakallu, Tariyakallu and such other towns of established fairs-..., Maddeya-dannayaka being the officer of Superintendence of the customs of our Fifty-six countries,- we confer upon him the mayoralty of the earth, and grant him one *svamya..*". [34]

The Keladi inscriptions give details about the goods that were traded in South Kanara. An inscription belonging to A.D.1641 from Tirthahalli, mentions the freedom from the bullock tax given by Virabhadra Nayaka for the Mahattu *math* built by Durga Timmanna. The inscription mentions the following: "in the kingdom that we are ruling, in the *tanes* above the ghats, for the *matha,* 5 bullocks,-except tassels, silk, arecanut, pepper, cocoanut kernels and wood,-laden with bamboo baskets, grain, rice, paddy, ragi, salt, jaggory, oil, ghee and other such articles."[35] Another inscription dated A.D.1673 refers to a grant given by Chennammaji for the Mahattu *math* of Jeni on the road from Bidarur to Kumbasi. This record states the following: "Freedom from tolls on 5 bullocks for the above matha - except arecanut, pepper, tassels, silk, cocoa-nut kernels, wood and such other goods for gain- laden with rice, paddy, ragi, oil, ghee, fruit, jaggory, rattan and such articles, on registering the colour and age of the bullocks in the customs *thanes* below the Ghats in the Ikkeri-hobli".[36]

Another inscription belonging to A.D.1711 mentions a grant for the Mahattu *math* by Basavappa Nayaka as follows: "We remit the toll on 25 bullocks - except arecanut, pepper, tassels, silk, wood and other goods for gain- laden with rice, paddy, ragi, salt, acid, rattan, grain, oil, ghi, pulse, jaggory, fruit, cutch, cocoa-nut kernels, cloths, iron, dates, tobacco, asafoetida, cumin seed, mustard, fenugreek, onion, garlic turmeric, ginger and other such articles- on the colour and ages of bullocks being registered in the customs *thanes* in Durga, Ikkeri and the *hobalis* below the Ghats".[37] Thus these inscriptions give a list of items that were traded between South Kanara and the ghat region.[38] However, they do not tell anything about the places of production, value, quantity and nature of exchange of these goods.

In the Chola domain, *nagaram* commercial centres provided the setting for market-oriented exchange of goods and services. Such centres had streets of permanent shops where exchanges were continuously transacted.[39] In the case of South Kanara too we come across the *angadi* and other commercial terms. Two inscriptions dated Saka 1371 mention *nakhara* of Baindur with the existence of *angadi.*[40] It is evident from these inscriptions that Baindur was a commercial centre during the fourteenth century itself.

Kenneth R. Hall has made a study of the relations between the local market and the itinerant trade in the context of the Chola period. He says that the *nagaram* towns functioned as points of redistribution where certain commodities of foreign origin were made available for the local *nadu's* consumption. The local economic networks in turn were serviced by itinerant trade groups who specialised in exotic commodities ranging from gems to elephants. The itinerants depended upon an assortment of relationships beyond the coastal ports to support their commercial activities. Their local presence may be characterised as of three types: (i) itinerant merchants inhabited a specified and permanent quarter of a commercial centre; (ii) itinerant merchants occasionally visited a community and were thus rightfully described as part-time residents; (iii) itinerant merchant organisations incorporated local merchants into their membership as the local merchant became the itinerant organisation's local trade representative.[41]

In South Kanara too one can identify the relations between the local trader and the itinerant trader. There are references in the inscriptions to the itinerant traders making grants to the temple and while doing so they took the consent of local trade guilds and other important assemblies of the locality. In South Kanara some of the traders belonged to Hinduism. Among them the Gowda Sarasvats were prominent. They had their contacts with Goa. There existed historical and cultural relations between South Kanara and Goa. In both places similar traditions regarding the establishment of brahman settlements by Parashurama exist. The Kadambas of Goa were a branch of the Kadambas of Karnataka. The Sarasvat traders of Goa had trade contacts with South Kanara. When the Portuguese came to Goa in the 16th century and later pursued the policy of religious conversion, some of the Sarasvats migrated to South Kanara and settled in this region permanently. They invested their money in land and other commercial enterprises in South Kanara and made land and money grants to the temples. For instance, the Gangolli inscription belonging to A.D.1662 mentions that Bhadrappa Nayaka endowed *umbali* land in the Gangolli village of Muguvina *sime* to Narayana Mallya who hailed from the Gove *rajya* in Jayavarni *grama.* Narayana Mallya installed Venkataramana deity in the Gangolli village and the temple is called Mallera *matha.*[42] This helped them to gain popularity among the local populace and they were well versed in the local language, namely, Kannada and they have left records in Kannada as found in the Goa Archives and the Mhamai House records.[43]

The studies conducted by James Heitzman on South India have shown that in the Tamil region the expansion of local temples occurred alongside the expansion of commercial networks focused on the mercantile communities (*nagaram*) sprinkled amid the numerous agrarian zones. The early *nagaram* were the heart of small scale exchange networks in some basic commodities, manufactured articles and luxury goods, which penetrated even to the rural community level. Temple rituals demanded a wide collection of food items and precious commodities, many of which required the services of merchants for procurement and artisans or specialized workers for fabrication into complex contributions and cult objects. Specialists in commerce and manufacturing lived beside the Brahman ritual specialists, the cultivating groups and the farming labourers congregated in large number around the lands of the religious institutions.[44] As in the Tamil region and other parts of South India, in South Kanara too the traders were required to render certain services. They contributed to the emergence of towns in different localities through the exchange of agrarian and craft products. They also gave land grants and administered them. Thus trade was the basic prerequisite for urbanisation in certain areas. Scholars like Champakalakshmi have tried to highlight the role of royal power in the process of urbanisation, particularly in the administrative centres. But the royalty was not in a position to extend this process to the different parts of the empire and that too the peripheral regions. This work was left to the mercantile and agricultural communities of the locality. In this area also we find close collaboration between the agrarian and trading communities of South Kanara. Because both these communities produced commodities which were sold in the local markets. Similarly the role played by the traders of South Kanara in the emergence of temple-based or religion-based urban centres was considerable. Almost all the major towns of the region such as Mangalore, Barkur, Basrur, Baindur, Gangolli and Karkala gave shelter to traders trading in different goods, agricultural and non-agricultural. People of the locality sold and purchased the items as required by them. The devotees who visited the temples or *basadis* or *maths* constituted another major group of customers at the temple-based towns. Besides the annual festivals in the various religious institutions provided opportunities for the exchange of a large variety of goods in considerable quantities in the *jatres.* In these *jatres* one could see not only the permanent shops but also a large number of temporary shops selling goods, eatables and musical instruments and play items.

Muslim Traders in South Kanara

There existed Muslim settlements in South Kanara. It is said that the Muslim colony of Honnavar in North Kanara, which was governed by Jalal-ud-din was the progenitor of the enterprising Muhammadan community in Kanara known as Navayats. The word Navayat means newcomers. On their arrival in India, these refugees took to commerce, and before long came to have the whole of the coastal trade in their hands. They had their settlement in Barkur as described by Ibn Batuta. The menace of the Muslim pirates on the coast of Barkur forced the Hoysala king Vira Ballala III to post his general Ankeya Nayaka there.[45]

The Arab traders maintained regular contacts with the Western coast. The boats of the Arabs used to come to Malabar and other coastal areas of India sometime in July or August and after about four months of business returned in December or January. In those days the voyage used to take about thirty to forty days. So even if the Arab sailors and merchants had any settled home life in Arabia, they were away from their homes for the major part of the year. Thus while they were in India they must have contracted marital unions, temporary or permanent with the Indian women, for there is no evidence to show that they brought along with them their own womenfolk.[46] The folk songs of South Kanara, the *paddanas* like Ali Bhuta Bobbariya give information about the settlements of Arab traders and their matrimonial relations with local women in the regions of Manjesvara, Barkur, Basrur and Murudesvara. Some of the Tulu *paddanas* allude to the nature of the Arab trading activities in the coastal towns where they settled down, and carried on brisk trade transactions in rice, pepper, coir, ginger, etc. in exchange for vessels from China, varieties of silk clothes, dried fruits, fine breeds of horses and large quantities of Persian and European gold. They came into contact with the various guilds like *settikaras, elamegalu* and *nakharas.*[47]

The Navayats of Kanara were found along the coastal strip between the Sharavati river in North Kanara and the Suvarna river in South Kanara. Their settlements were invariably situated either by the seashore mainly at the mouth of rivers or a little interior on the banks of the rivers so that in any case they have an easy access to the sea. In South Kanara they were found in Sirur, Baindoor, Gangolli, Basrur, Kandlur, Hangarkatte, Bengare, Tonse and Malpe.[48]

Victor S. D' Souza stated that owing to the special facilities that were obtainable at Malabar, the Arab traders first established their colonies there and from there carried on their trade with other convenient places. Enterprising merchants settled down for longer period at places advantageous to their trade. These temporary settlements eventually developed into small colonies. These colonies were patronised by the Muslim merchants who came directly from Arabia and Persia.[49] Some of these settlements like Mangalore and Bhatkal developed later into trading centres and facilitated the process of urbanisation.

Both Arabic and Indian sources allude to the existence of Indian trade centres in Arabia and *vice versa.* Ubla near Basra, Mecca, Petre, Baghdad, Oman, Dubai, Sanas, Aden, etc. were the prominent Indian trade centres in the Arab world, whereas Nilesvara, Kasaragod, Kumbla, Mangalore, Manel, Mukka,

Yermal, Muluru, Barkur, Basrur and Bhatkal were the Arab trade centres in coastal Karnataka. The traded commodities of the Arabs in these places were swords, silk, textiles, wood, ginger, spices and various kinds of medicines.[50] Sturrock mentioned the trading communities of South Kanara among whom Mapillas and Navayats were the major groups. The other trading castes were the Banajigas, Balijas, Chettis and Vaisyas. Balijas was the well-known Telugu trading caste and Banajiga was the Kannada form of this name. Trade was also carried on by Gowda Saraswat Brahmins, native Christians, Rajapuris and Vanis. The Vanis had come to South Kanara from Goa and they spoke Konkani language.[51]

The above study shows that in South Kanara there was the emergence of a powerful trading group which participated in the trade both internal and external. As a result there was the establishment of commercial contact with the outside world. The traders were able to earn enormously in the form of profits and they were in a position to wield considerable influence in political, economic and social spheres. They caused the construction of religious monuments and contributed to the urbanisation of the locality.[52]

Guilds

As in other parts of India, in South Kanara also we could see the existence of guilds. Populous trade centres like Barkur, Basrur and Mudabidre had their trade or merchant guilds called *nakhara* (*nakharadavaru*), *settikara* and *hanjamana*. Among these *nakhara* can be compared with *nagarattar* of the Tamil region. According to K. V. Ramesh *nakhara* is to be understood in the sense of 'merchant community' or 'guild of merchants' or 'a mercantile town'. *Settikara* is derived from the word Setti meaning merchant or trader. While *settikara* was the association of native merchants who dealt in indigenous commodities, the *nakhara* was the guild of native merchants who were concerned with overseas trade.[53]

Hanjamana guild existed and flourished in South Kanara from the days of the Alupas. A record of A.D. 1114 from Barkur says that the *nagara* and *hanjamana* of Barkur were present in the king's court when he made a grant to Markandesvara temple.[54] Indigenous organisations like the *nakhara, nakhara-hanjamanas* and the *settikaras* were associated with the Hoysala administration. The Hoysala inscriptions from South Kanara mention *settikaras* in specific number such as *nalvaru settikararu, entu praje settikararu*, a feature which became more common in Vijaynagara inscriptions. The Hoysala inscriptions also mention about the subdivision of *nadu.* This did not figure in the earlier inscriptions. The Hiriyangadi inscription dated A.D.1334 refers to *nadu* and *nakhara* of Karkal. It also mentions the *halaru* of Karkal and *ubhayananadesigalu.* The *halaru* guild was generally considered to be made up of persons belonging to different professions. The *nanadesis* were active in all regions without limits of the political boundary. There is reference to *ubhayananadesis.* It is suggested that *ubhaya* is to be taken as denoting local (*svadesi*) and foreign (*paradesi*) merchant communities.[55]

The Mudabidre inscription refers to *salikeya aruvaru ballalugalu* and *aivaru horahinavaru* (five *ballalas* of *salike* and five outsiders). According to Kittel *salike* means 'business in a room or shop'. It may be suggested that the *salikeya ballalugalu* were members of the guild of businessmen, who were considered as citizens of importance. *Horahinavaru* means outsiders. They were connected with *salike* but hailed from outside the Tuluva region. It may be that they secured the *ballalu* traders commodities from outside the Tulu country.[56] A record from Barkur dated A.D. 1335-36 speaks of *nakhara-hanjamana* of Barkur. The Hoysala queen Kikkayitayi made a grant of the whole revenue from the village Bailur to one person by name Vasudeva Mudali. For this she sought the permission of the general assembly of *nakhara-hanjamana* of the place. [57]

During the Vijayanagara period we find large number of inscriptions which mention the existence of *hanjamanas* in various trade centres like Ullal, Basrur and Mangalore. Suryanath Kamath believed that "they were Muslim organisations because clearly there is reference to *pallis* in the inscriptions".[58] But *palli* might also have meant a village and not necessarily the Muslim mosque. According to K.V. Ramesh they were the organisation of the Parsee and Arab traders.[59] Thus we can say they were the guild of the foreign traders who came to South Kanara from Arab countries.

In the Vijayanagara period the importance of *hanjamana* guild increased due to the emergence of horse trade. The Vijayanagara kings demanded a large number of horses (both dead and alive) from foreign traders. According to K.P.Poonacha and M.V. Viswesvara, with the sole intention of gaining direct control over the region and to centralise the horse trade the Vijayanagara kings established new territorial divisions like Barkur-*vishaya*, Honnavar-*vishaya,* Mangalore *rajya* etc. These places had regular administrative offices established obviously for the effective economic and supervisory control over the trade activities.[60]

The *hanjamana* guilds were also categorised as *ubhaya nanadesis.* They were associated with inland as well as external trade, in the capacity of *vinimaya vartakasangha* (exchange-guilds), with well established colonies. Though epigraphs are silent as to the exact commodities that these people used to handle, we can suggest that they mainly traded in horses. It was quite possible that the *hanjamana* guild enjoyed influence due to the immense fortune accumulated by individual merchants from the trade of horses.[61] Even the local principalities were interested in horse trade. According to ***Gomatesvara Charitre,*** Virapandya of Karkal procured horses from Vanayaja, Kambhoja and Bahlika.[62]

The Vijayanagara rulers had import war horses from Arabia and such other lands. Therefore, the Vijayanagara inscriptions of South Kanara make frequent references to *hanjamana* and *nakhara-hanjamana* guilds and their activities.[63] Repeated references to these guilds indicate the enhanced importance of horse trade in the Vijayanagara empire. They also reflect the pivotal role played by the *hanjamanas* in the trading activities. *Hanjamanas* were found even in the interior trade centres. For instance a copy of the inscription belonging to the period of Keladi Somashekhar Nayak mentions the existence of *hallaru hanjamanaru* in Sringeri.[64]

In Barkur the guilds participated in the administration of the city. The *settis* formed themselves into guilds called *settikaras*. These guilds dealt in varieties of commodities of daily consumption and articles of luxury. In Barkur there is a community called Settigaras. They live in groups in Barkur, Salikeri, Suratkal, Mangalore and other places. There are eighteen prominent settlements of this community in South Kanara. B. Vasantha Shetty has suggested that there is similarity in the names - Settikara and Settigara, and the transformation from Settikara to Settigara is quite possible.[65]

The ten *keris* of Barkur were represented by *halaru* and the sixteen *settikaras*. The *halaru* were the councillors of the town responsible for general administration. The sixteen *settikaras* of the ten *keris* were heads of the trade guilds.[66] The *gavares* were another community of traders who entrenched themselves in Barkur and Basrur. In Barkur they had set up their own temple known as *Gavaresvara-devalaya,* which was granted a gift of charity by one Annapa Setti.[67]

Another trade guild of South Kanara was *elamegalu*. Ballala III's inscription of A.D.1336, from Mudukeri in Barkur, mentions the *nura-aivattu*(150)*elame*. His Mudabidre inscription of A.D.1342 refers to *nalvaru*(4) *elamegalu*. The fact that *elame* was a guild or an association with its own binding regulations to the members is attested by the reference in many Vijayanagara inscriptions to the phrase *elamege olagadavaru* or those who were involved in *elame*. The figures 150 or 4 probably pertain to different guilds with the common name of *elame*.[68] The *elame* in Venur was connected with number three hundred and sixty four while in the *hattukeri* of Barkur it was seven hundred and seventy.[69]

The collective work of Jain guilds is depicted in the inscriptions of Mudabidre belonging to Hoysala and Vijayanagara periods. The *Hosa basadi* (new temple), also called the thousand pillared *basadi* bears ample testimony to this. Even the *basadis* here were named after their builders like *Settara basadi,* Vikarama-Setti *basadi,* Madiah-Setti *basadi,* Mahadeva-Setti *basadi* and Chola-Setti *basadi.* P.N. Narasimha Murthy opined that there was a kind of competition among the merchants to build large number of *basadis.*[70] The spirit of competition might have existed among the wealthy merchants who wanted to create memorials to exhibit their socio-economic status. But it was basically the belief in religion that influenced the Jain merchants to construct *basadis.*

Some scholars have discussed about the significance of donations to the temple. For example, James Hietzman rightly said that the people who could afford to give lavish gifts to religious institutions, and then arrange to engrave the memory of their beneficence, were often members of the most important cultural, political and economic elites in their societies. The driving force behind donations was the concept of legitimisation of authority, whereby gifts to gods or representatives on earth resulted in a transfer of divine sanctity and the merit to the givers.[71] The factor of legitimisation of authority also probably made the Jain merchants of South Kanara to build *basadis*

According to K.R.Hall *nagaram* merchants were often contracted to make certain specified goods and services available to their local temple and community in exchange for house-sites or exemption from certain taxes.[72] Kenneth Hall quotes from George Spencer who suggested that "the redistribution of royal revenues *via* gifts to temples was part of a conscious attempt to forge links with the countryside."[73] Numerous grants of tolls, duties and commercial products were made by various *nagarams* without any evident outside pressure. *Nagarams* are most conspicuous in their involvement with local temple administration. Temple funds were commonly entrusted to a *nagaram* for investment.[74] K. R. Hall wrote that it was not strange to find the *nagaram*, the community's commercial elite, involved in temple finances. The Chola rulers attempted to penetrate the local village political domain by establishing royal control over the hinterland temples.[75] The relations between *nagaram* and temples that existed during the Chola period seem to have prevailed in South Kanara too. If the nature and magnitude of their functioning were more established and developed in the Chola state, in South Kanara they were less advanced.

The trade guilds apart from their economic role, performed the role of administrators of towns, gave donations to the temples and looked after the property of the temples, and had very close relation with the state. There existed the trade guilds like *hanjamana, nakhara, settikara, elame, halaru, nanadesi* and *ubhayananadesi.*

An inscription belonging to A.D. 1444 mentions that the *nakharas* and *settis* of Dharmapattana agreed to pay to the temple of Mahadeva a portion of toll-revenue raised in the village. It was to be used for the repair of gold pinnacle of the temple and the balance, if any, was to be used for the services of god and for no other purpose. The gift was made to expiate the sin committed by them in having murdered two men of their community.[76] The outside traders who came to South Kanara made land donations. An inscription belonging to Saka year 1281 refers to one Bankarasa from Hubli making grants to Somanatha temple at Barkur.[77] An inscription belonging to Saka year 1334 mentions Jogi Setti of Arikana Ghatta of Nagamangala who made some grants to the temple.[78] One inscription from Barkur mentions the relations that existed between *Hattukeriya Halaru* and Karkal.[79] Both Barkur and Karkal were Jain centres. The fact that urban culture was developing not only in the core areas like Barkur and Basrur but also in a periphery like Shankaranarayana is proved by the inscription belonging to A.D. 1562 which mentions the existence of *angadi* or shop in Shankaranarayana.[80]

Barkur inscription belonging to Saka year 1282 mentions that Naganna Setti gave some donations to the temple. If Naganna Setti was not able to give the promised money, it was the responsibility of *Murukeriya Halaru* to make Naganna Setti to give money. This implies that Naganna Setti was a member of *halaru* and before making any grant he was supposed to seek the permission of *halaru.*[81] The Barkur inscription of Saka year 1508 mentions *manigara keriya halara gadi* (*gadi* means the boundary), which means that this guild was the owner of some property.[82] An inscription found in the Krishna *math* of Udupi of Saka year 1359 mentions that the Governor Annappa Odeya attacked Sivalli grama. The trade guilds of Barkur tried to pacify the Brahmans by giving land grants to them.[83]

The Basrur inscription of A.D. 1554 mentions that Timmayya Setti purchased a plot of land and constructed a *math.* He purchased a *brahmadaya* land from Anna Udupa and made a gift of the same for the maintenance of the *chatra* attached to the *math.*[84] An inscription belonging to Keladi period states that if money was not received from a place called Anegali, then it was the responsibility of the *settikaras* to pay the money.[85]

The kings also gave grants to the temple. An inscription from Bantwala Muda, Mangalore Taluk, which belongs to A.D. 1364 states that under the orders of the king, Madarasa of Mangalore made a gift of the village Pudugrama, to certain Brahmans. This edict also mentions the *nakharadavaru.*[86] The presence of *nakhara* in the royal edict indicates the respect given to the traders while giving the land grant. An inscription belonging to A.D. 1451 mentions that under the orders of Devaraya-Maharaya, Bhanappa-Odeya who was ruling over Barkur-rajya, made a gift of 121 *kati-gadyanas* out of the *siddhaya* of Basrur, for the service of god Nakharesvaradeva of the place.[87] God Nakharesvara was the personal deity of the traders of Barkur. By giving grants to this temple the kings were seeking the support of traders. The Basrur inscription of A.D. 1444 mentions that the several *settikaras* of Paduvakeri in Basrur gave land grants to Narana-Setti for offerings and service in the temple of Nakharesvara.[88]

The traders used to go on pilgrimage. The Basrur inscription dated A.D. 1472 mentions that Duggana-Setti of Paduvakeri at Basrur and his three nephews made a grant of land to Siriyappa on the latter's return from his pilgrimage to Benaras for the worship of the image of god Kasi-Visvanatha which he had brought with him.[89]

The *hanjamanas* paid tax to the state. An inscription belonging to A.D. 1465 records that when Pandarideva Odeya was ruling over Barkur-rajya, he made a gift of gold, which the *Hanjamana* community was paying, for the service of god Mahadeva at Paduvakeri, on the occassion of a lunar eclipse.[90]

Sometimes there occurred conflicts between the traders. The Basrur inscription belonging to A.D. 1455[91] records that an agreement was effected between the settis of the two streets, namely, Paduvakeri and Mudakeri in Basrur. It was regarding the boundaries and the rights of their respective localities, and the paths through which the settis of each locality had to take sheep and arecanut trees to the temple of Devi on occasions of festivals.

The significance of the inscription lies in the amicable settlement made by the people themselves to avoid conflicts on matters regarding property and the religion. It mentions the roads used by *sudeshi* and *paradesi*. Perhaps this points out the existence of indigenous traders and foreign (outside) traders. Whenever dispute arose between the traders, the rulers tried to create a peaceful atmosphere by making traders to sign agreement.

The Barkur inscription belonging to Saka year 1353 mentions that there arose a conflict between traders of Mudukeri and Chaulikeri regarding the trade in sugar. The conflict also resulted from a controversy over the utilisation of crops and other groceries coming from beyond the ghats. Since the controversy had resulted in armed fights, the governor summoned to his court the five *halaru* of Chaulikeri and the *samastahalaru* of Murukeri and effected a compromise between the contending groups. They accordingly undertook never again to use violence in settling their differences. This agreement stipulated a separate place for the foreign merchants in the warehouse where they had to store their goods. The inscription mentions the import of goods like rice, wheat, Bengal gram, Phaseolus mungo (*uddu*), green gram (*hesaru*), sesamum indicum (*ellu*), sugar-cane (*kabbu*), fenugreek (*mente*), ghee (*tuppa*) and jaggery (*bella*). This record also prescribes certain regulations for the sale of sugar brought by the local and foreign merchants from above the ghats. It states that merchants of Chaulikeri and Murukeri should collectively weigh and store the stock of sugar and that whatever quantity remained unsold should not be taken to Murukeri by the merchants of that part of the city but should remain in the storehouse to be sold in times of demand. This clause was included to maintain the balance in the trade and to control the fluctuation in the price. The right of selling cotton sarees was made the exclusive privilege of merchants of Murukeri.[92]

An inscription from Chokkadi, Udupi Taluk, belonging to A.D. 1474 mentions about a dispute which arose over certain lands in Vodevuru between the *settikaras* of *hattukeri* of Barkur and the *nakhara-hanjamanas* on the one side and Nidamburas, Mudilas and six ballalas on the other. It was settled in the favour of the former.[93]

Sometimes there emerged misunderstanding between the trade guilds and the rulers. The Mangalore inscription belonging to Saka year 1341 informs us that when Timmanna Odeya was ruling Mangaluru *rajya*, while *hanjamana-nakhara* were giving *poorva mariyade,* Timmanna Odeya became angry with them and destroyed their villages by sending his army. This news reached Dannayaka Bayicheddannayaka Odeya who was staying on the other bank of the river and made arrangements to redress the grievances of the *hanjamana-nakhara* by granting them some of the villages in Kodeyala (Mangalore). Timmanna Odeya discussed this matter with his Pradhani, Bangas, Chautas, Ajilas and *samastha kattale.*[94] The Barkur inscription of A.D. 1406 states that injustice was done to *hanjamana-nakhara* by Mahabaladeva. In order to redress their grievance king Bukkaraya sent Bachanna of Goa who came to Barkur *rajya* and he gave certain land for the purchase of cloth by the trade guilds. This inscription shows that the kings took personal interest in comforting the traders. This also indicates the influence that the traders enjoyed with the kings.[95]

In North Kanara also there occurred the misunderstanding between the Governor and the *hanjamana*. A serious breach occurred between the Governor Timmanna Odeya and one Ummara-Marakala, the chief of the *hanjamana* of Honnavar. The latter, along with his supporters, retired to Kasarakodu and appealed to Sangiraya Odeya, the chief of Nagire for help. On receiving this appeal, Sangiraya dispatched one Kotisvara-nayaka, along with thousand soldiers, to offer protection to Ummara-Marakala and his followers.[96] Thus Ummara -Marakala used the good offices of the chief of Nagire and brought about the cessation of the hostilities that the Governor had against him. This shows that some times there emerged conflicts between the merchants and the state officials during this period. Generally the interest of the traders was well protected.

The traders were expected to follow certain rules in society. The traders were a part of *balanju*. The Alupa inscription of Mangalore (dateless) mentions that if Setti committed a sin or a mistake the punishment was that he was to be excommunicated from the *balanju*.[97] An inscription from Mudabidre (dateless) mentions about an agreement signed by *settikaras, elamegalu, nadu* and *nakhara* according to which they punished those traders who violated *balanju niti*. Those who violated this rule were made to pay one *talesavira honnu*.[98]

There are references to the items that were traded and the description of the urbanity of the cities like Mudabidre. An inscription of Saka year 1351 gives some details about Mudabidre. Vamsapura or Venupura (Mudabidre) is described as a place where there existed trade in *ratna kanchana chinambara*. Chinambara was the silk cloth brought from China. It also refers to Venupura's *Yentupraje Settikararu Nalvaru Elamegolagada Samasta Halaru* who gave land as per the instruction of Devaraya Maharaya to Charukirti Panditadevaru for the construction of *chaityalaya* called Tribhuvana Chudamani.[99]

One inscription of Mudabidre states the patronage given by *halaru settikaras* for the construction of second storey of the Jain monument Tribhuvana Chudamani in Mudabidre.[100]

Another inscription belonging to Saka year 1373 mentions the name of several Settis who were responsible for the wonderful construction of the *mukhamantapa* of Tribhuvana Chudamani.[101] This inscription gives an idea of the social set up of Mudabidre. It is possible that most of these Settis mentioned in the inscription were the landlords belonging to Bunt community but later with the arrival of Jainism they might have been converted into Jainism and they donated for the construction of Jain monuments. They followed the *aliya santana*, the usual practice of inheritance of property from the mother's side, prevailing among the Bunts of South Kanara. The references to the names of nephews clearly indicate the matrilineal pattern of society. The above inscription mentions certain names like Alva Narana Setti and Kajava Devaru Setti. These names clearly indicate that originally they were Bunts and later they were converted into Jainism. They gave grants to both Jain and Brahmanical temples. The conversion to Jainism was also due to the fact that Jainism was a more suitable religion for the trading community who had to violate the taboos of the brahmanical religion. Jainism did not impose any restriction on crossing the sea and participating in trade. Religion was a binding force for the Jain traders.

Large number of donations were made to Tribhuvana Chudamani. In Saka year 1384 *nalkuru ayinura saviradavaru* of Barkur made land donations to Tribhuvana Chudamani. The *Halaru Settikaras* were entrusted with the responsibility of protecting this grant.[102] Another Mudabidre inscription gives list of people who were responsible for the construction of the third storey of Tribhuvana Chudamani.[103]

The traders were given certain privileges. For instance an inscription belonging to Saka year 1500 mentions that with the consent of *settikaras nalvaru elamegolagada samasta halaru* and by the order of Charukirti Panditadevaru, no other houses should be constructed to the east of Mainda's house. Those who committed this mistake should pay 1200 *varahas* to the Chautas of Mudabidre.[104]

During the pre-twelfth century period townships were

designated *nagara* or *nakhara, pura* and *pattana.* We have references to Udayapura *nakhara* and *Mangalapura-mahanagara.* Some of the early Alupa inscriptions refer to *padinentu pattana* (eighteen towns). K. V. Ramesh opined that this phrase refers to the administrative bodies in the eighteen cities.[105]

During the Vijayanagara period, guilds and local assemblies were more frequently entrusted with the task of protecting and administering gifts and grants made to temples. This is indicated in expressions such as *Chaulikeriyalli muvaru settikararu halaru pratipalisuvaru,* (three *settikaras* administer in Chaulikeri), *i dharmada parupatya odetana kotekeriya halaru settikararige* (this grant should be managed and owned by *halaru settikaras* of Kotekeri), etc. which are very often seen in the records of this period.[106] Above details show that trades and trade guilds actively participated in the process of construction of temples and maintenance of temple grants. Thus political, economic and religious factors were at work in the process of urbanisation in South Kanara.

Notes and References

1. K. R. Hall, ***Trade and Statecraft in the Age of Cholas***, *Op. Cit*, P. 1.
2. *Grahapatis* were the landlords who also participated in long distance trade in ancient India. See Romila Thapar, ***From Lineage to State Social Formations in the Mid-First Millennium B.C. in the Ganga Valley,*** Delhi, 1990, P. 36.
3. ***Epigraphia Indica*** Vol. IX, P.22.
4. *Ibid*, P.23.
5. ***SII,*** Vol. IX, Part I, No.578.
6. Syed Abdul Bari, "**Non-Agrarian Taxation in Karnataka Under Vijayanagara (1336-1565)**, *Op. Cit*, P.29.
7. Sanjay Subrahmanyam, 'The Portuguese, the port of Basrur and Rice Trade 1600-50', in S.Subrahmanyam (Ed.), ***Merchants, Markets and the State in Early Modern India***, *Op. Cit*, PP. 25-26.

8. Syed Abdul Bari, *Op. Cit.,* PP. 32-34.
9. *Ibid.*
10. ***SII,*** Vol. IX, Part II, No.459.
11. ***SII,*** Vol. VII, No.247.
12. ***ARSIE,*** 1931-32, No.3.
13. ***SII,*** Vol. VII, No.450.
14. A. K.Shastry, "**Selections From the Kaditas of the Sringeri Matha**", Unpublished ICHR project report, 1982, P. 36.
15. ***Epigraphia Carnatica*** , VIII, Sagar, No. 123.
16. *Ibid.*
17. K. G. Vasanthamadhava, ***Western Karnataka-Its Agrarian Relations A.D. 1500-1800***, *Op. Cit,* P.200.
18. ***Epigraphia Carnatica*** , VIII, Tirthahalli, 42.
19. ***ARSIE***, 1939-40, No.14.
20. Y. Umanath Shenoy, ***Manjuvani***, Dharmasthala, 1989, P. 27.
21. K. G. Vasanthamadhava, ***Western Karnataka-Its Agrarian Relations A.D. 1500-1800***, Op. *Cit.,* P. 227.
22. A. K. Shastry, "**Records of the Shringeri Matha relating to Keladi**", Unpublished, Kadata 20, Record No. 27, Also see A. K. Shastry, " **Selections From the Kaditas of the Sringeri Matha**", *Op. Cit.,* P. 187.
23. Edward Grey, ***The Travels of Pietro Della Valle in India,*** Vol. II, *Op. Cit*, P. 304.
24. A. Subbanna Rai, ***Da. Ka. Jilleya Aitihyagalu*** (in Kannada), Bombay, 1994, P. 114.
25. ***Indian Antiquary,*** Vol. XXIII, PP. 151-152.
26. K. G. Vasanthamadhava, ***Western Karnataka-Its Agrarian Relations A.D. 1500-1800***, *Op. Cit.,* P. 137.
27. Mansel Longworth Dames (Ed.), ***The Book of Duarte Barbosa***, *Op. Cit*, P.192, PP.195-196.
28. K. G. Vasanthamadhava, ***Western Karnataka-Its Agrarian Relations A.D. 1500-1800***, *Op. Cit.,* P. 139.

29. *Ibid.*

30. Y. Umanath Shenoy, 'Shasanavondaralli belakige banda ajnata rani Shankaradevi Ajila' (in Kannada), in, ***Udayavani***, 4-1-98.

31. ***E.C.,*** VIII, Sorab, 467.

32. ***E.C., N.S.,*** IX, Belur, 181.

33. Shripad Rama Sharma, 'Vijayanagara and Jainism', ***Vijayanagara Sexcentenary Commemmoration Volume***, Dharwar, 1936, P. 71.

34. ***E.C.***, ***N.S.,*** IX, Belur, No. 171. For details of the *muleya svamya* (custom duty), see **APPENDIX – I.**

35. ***E.C.,***VIII, Tirthahalli, No. 49.

36. *Ibid,* Tirthahalli, No. 68.

37. *Ibid,* Tirthahalli, No. 72.

38. For inscriptions giving similar details see, *Ibid,* Tirthahalli Nos. 84, 89, 92 and 184.

39. Kenneth R. Hall, *Op. Cit.,* P. 105.

40. K. G. Vasanthamadhava, 'Baindurina Eradu Shilasasanagala Adhyayana', in, ***Itihasa Darshana*** (in Kannada), Bangalore, 1995, PP. 144-145.

41. Kenneth R. Hall, 'Price-making and Market Hierarchy in Early Medieval South India' in Sanjay Subrahmanyam (Ed.), ***Money and Market in India 1100-1700***, *Op. Cit*, PP. 77-82.

42. K. G. Vasanthamadhava, ***Trends in Karnataka Historical Research***, Mangalore, 1996, P. 29.

43. Teotonio R. de Souza, 'Mhamai House Records: Indigenous Sources for Indo-Portuguese Historiography', ***The Indian Archives,*** Vol. XXXI, January-June, 1982, No. 1, PP. 25-45.

44. James Heitzman, *Op. Cit.,* P. 109.

45. George M. Moraes, 'Haryab of Ibn Batuta', ***Journal of Bombay Branch of Royal Asiatic Society,*** N.S., Vol. 15, 1939, P. 37.

46. Victor S. D' Souza, ***The Navayats of Kanara A Study in Culture Contact***, Dharwar, 1955, P.4.

47. K. G. Vasanthamadhava, 'Karnataka's Trade with the Arab world (c. 9th-18th century A.D.)'***Quarterly Review of Historical Studies***,

Vol. XXXVI, April-Sept 1996, Nos. 1&2, P.30. These guilds will be discussed in the next section.

48. Victor S. D' Souza, *Op. Cit.,* P. 35.

49. *Ibid,* PP. 54-55.

50. K. G. Vasanthamadhava, 'Karnataka's Trade with the Arab World', *Op. Cit.,* P. 29.

51. Sturrock,*Op. Cit*, PP. 155-156.

52. In South India the role of traders, trade guilds and urbanisation have been studied by Meera Abraham, *Op. Cit.,* 1988 and R. Champakalakshmi, ***Trade, Ideology and Urbanization South India 300 B.C. to A.D. 1300,*** *Op. Cit.*

53. K.V.Ramesh, ***A History of South Kanara,*** *Op. Cit., P.* 252

54. ***SII,*** Vol. VII, No. 380.

55. K. V. Ramesh, *Op. Cit.,* P. 255-56.

56. *Ibid,* P. 256.

57. ***ARSIE,*** 1929-30, No. 528.

58. Suryanath U. Kamath, 'Hanjamana', ***The Journal of Institute of Asian Studies,*** Vol. I, No. 1, May 1978, P. 60.

59. K. V. Ramesh, *Op. Cit.,* P. 253.

60. K. P. Poonacha and M.V. Viswesvara, 'Vijayanagar Port-Towns of Karnataka with Special Reference to Horse Trade', S.R.Rao (Ed.) ***The Role of Universities and Research Institutes in Marine Archaeology,*** Goa, 1994, P. 84.

61. *Ibid,* P. 85.

62. Y. Umanath Shenoy, ***Karkalada Sri Gomatesvara Charitre***, Ujire, 1991, P. 23.

63. K. V.Ramesh, *Op. Cit.,* P. 253.

64. A.K. Shastry, **"Selections From the Kaditas of the Sringeri Matha"**, *Op. Cit.,* P. 210.

65. B Vasantha Shetty, *Op. Cit.,* P. 336.

66. P. Gururaja Bhat , ***Studies in Tuluva History and Culture*** *Op. Cit*, P. 171.

67. *Ibid,* P. 217.

68. K. V. Ramesh, *Op. Cit.,* P. 257.

69. A. V. Venkataratnam, ***Local Government in the Vijayanagara Empire***,*Op. Cit,* P. 121.

70. P. N. Narasimha Murthy, *Op. Cit.,* P. 477.

71. James Hietzman, *Op. Cit,* P.1.

72. Kenneth R. Hall, *Op. Cit.,* P.71.

73. George W. Spencer, 'Temple Money-Lending and Livestock Redistribution', ***IESHR,*** Vol. 5, No. 3, 1968, PP. 286-287, quoted in Kenneth R. Hall, *Op. Cit,*P. 72.

74. Kenneth R. Hall, *Op. Cit.,* P. 76.

75. *Ibid,* P. 79.

76. ***SII*,** Vol. VII, No. 450.

77. *Ibid*, No. 330.

78. *Ibid,* No. 310.

79. *Ibid,* No. 314.

80. *Ibid*, Vol. IX Part II, No.674.

81. ***SII*** Vol. VII, No. 329.

82. *Ibid,* No. 331.

83. *Ibid,* No.296.

84. *Ibid*, Vol. IX, Part II, No. 655.

85. *Ibid,* No. 683.

86. *Ibid,* No. 408.

87. *Ibid,* No. 456.

88. *Ibid,* No.449.

89. *Ibid,* No. 464.

90. *Ibid,* No. 459.

91. *Ibid* No. 457.

92. *Ibid,* Vol. VII, No.309 and 340. No. 309 was found in Murukeri and a copy of the same inscription was found in Chaulikeri.

93. ***ARSIE*** 1928-29, No. 502; K.V. Ramesh, ***A History of South Kanara*** *Op.Cit.,* P. 183.

94. ***SII,*** Vol. VII, No. 182.

95. *Ibid,* No. 349.

96. K.V. Ramesh, *Op. Cit.,* P. 196.

97. ***SII,*** Vol. VII, No. 185.

98. *Ibid,* No. 213.

99. *Ibid,* No. 196.

100. *Ibid,* No. 204.

101. *Ibid,* No. 197.

102. *Ibid,* No. 198.

103. *Ibid,* No. 206.

104. *Ibid,* Nos. 226 and 227.

105. K. V. Ramesh, *Op. Cit.,* P. 243.

106. *Ibid,* P. 305.

5
Ports, Transport, Market and Currency

Barkur

After the10th century A.D. Barkur emerged as an important trade centre in coastal Karnataka. Its importance was such that the Western Ghats came to be called *Barakanura Ghatta* (Barkur Ghat). The Barkur Ghat passed through the western boundary of Hoysala empire.[1] It had all conveniences to develop as a centre of trade and commerce with a very deep river touching the town. The easy access to the sea helped Barkur to establish commercial contact with the outside world. Barkur got supplies, both for foreign trade as well as for local consumption, from the upghat regions. It acted as a trans-shipment port and entrepot trade port. Entrepot trade port meant that the port received goods from other trade centres of different directions and the same cargo was exported to other regions. Usually the trade centres of Karnataka depended on the ports on western coast to export their goods to far away trade centres.

When compared with Udyavar, Barkur was located in a very convenient place and the latter had connections with the upghat region. This communication was possible through the Hosangadi Ghat. During the summer it was not a difficult job to cross the Varahi river. If they wanted to go through Agumbe Ghat there was no need for them to cross the river. Kokkarne and Chara slowly developed as trade centres and these places also could be very easily approached from Barkur. For all these, Udyavar was not so convenient. Udyavar had to face the problem of floods and this adversely affected the transport and communication network particularly during the monsoon. Barkur was situated in an elevated place and could not be visited by floods. Thus the strategic geographical location of Barkur cannot be ignored in its emergence as a political and

Major Rivers and Ports of South Kanara

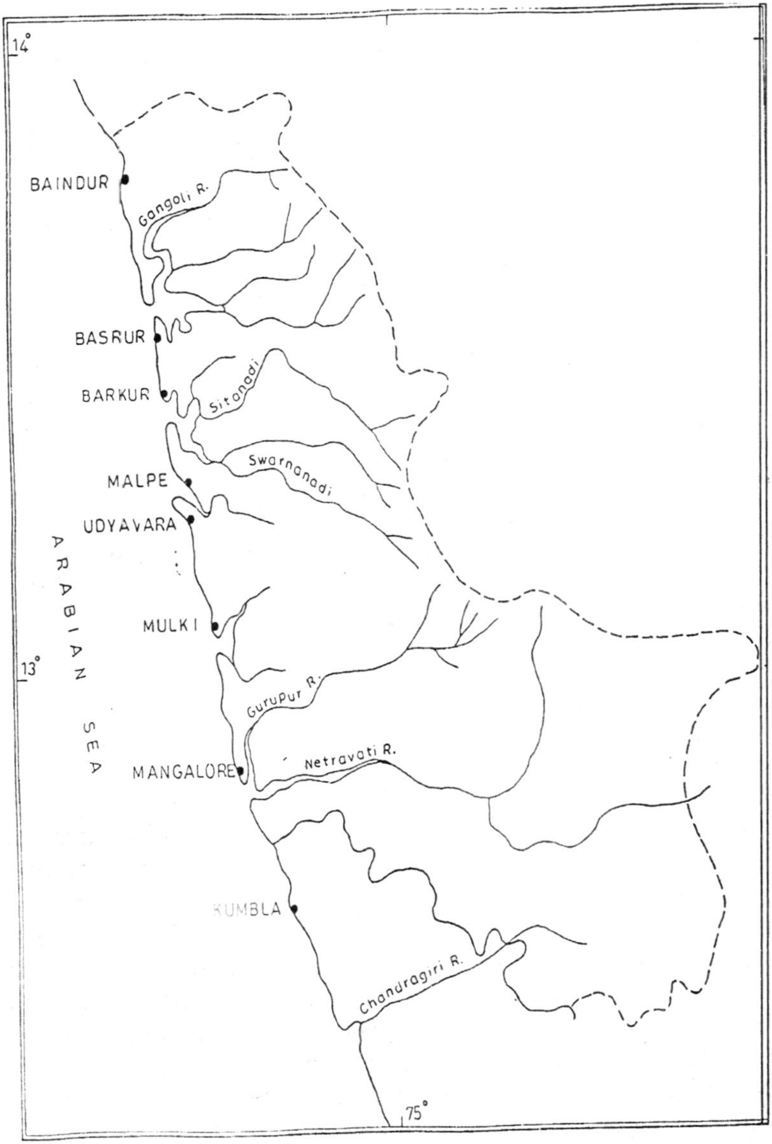

trading centre during the Alupa Period. The port of Barkur was very close to the town. This could help not only trade and commerce but also political contacts and defence. Basrur and Hattiyangadi could be reached either by water or land route. By the 12th century Udyavar lost its commercial importance. Thus, the Alupas in 12th century shifted their capital from Udyavar to Barkur.[2]

During this period South Kanara saw the emergence of a few urban centres. Due to the constant political patronage, Barkur emerged as an important urban centre. As a town busy in trade and commerce, Barkur had a developed municipal administration. *pattanaswami* (lord of town) was an important official in Barkur. The tenth century inscription discovered in Mudukeri refers to *pattanaswami* for the first time. It is said that *pattanaswami* constructed a *basadi* in Mudukeri. Another record of Soyideva Alupendra mentions "*pattanaswamiya hadi*" (forest of *pattanaswami*). Whenever the town was administered by different merchant guilds, the *pattanaswami* was the chief executor. In certain cities the number of *pattanaswami* was more than one. He was entrusted with the task of fixing the taxes to be paid by the townsmen. Conduct of fair was one of his main responsibilities.[3] An inscription from Nagar dated A.D. 1062 speaks of the works of Nokkaiah, the *Pattanaswami*. Nokkaiah is described as *Nakharamukha-mandana*. He is said to have constructed the Pattanaswami-Jinalaya, a tank, and caused to be made a number of images out of five metals.[4]

Barkur was divided into ten *keris* or quarters. But it seems that some of the *keris* were later additions and they might not have existed in the beginning. Probably with the extension and growth of the town it became necessary to add some more regions to the township and came to be considered as separate *keris* or quarters. Hosakeri or the new *keri* as the name itself suggests, might be a later addition. This also suggests the growth of the town and the changes that became necessary in its administration.[5] The Kotekeri inscription belonging to A.D. 1155 provides us the earliest reference to the municipal assembly. This inscription mentions *nagarasamuha* (administrators of the town).[6]

B. Vasantha Shetty accepted the suggestion of G.S. Dikshit that the parts of town began as streets but developed into quarters. The name *keri* was applied not only to a street but also to an area in Barkur. For example, *Balegara keri* (street of bangle sellers) stretched over an area much beyond a street. Each *keri* had its own reason for the name that it got. In extent also they differed from one another.[7]

Kotakeri got its name from the fort. This *keri* which also included the place now called old Barkur was the old commercial town of Barkur. This *keri* formed the port area and was an important centre of commercial activity. The weekly fair held now on Fridays seems to be a practice which has been continued from historical times. The fair must have contributed substantially to the growth of commercial activities of Barkur.[8] Balegarakeri had bangle sellers as the chief settlers.[9]

In Patasalakeri the community of weavers was dominant and the name Patasalaker*i* denotes the settlement of weavers.[10] B. Vasantha Shetty suggested that Manigarakeri was the street of dealers in gems and precious stones. But considering the possible limited demand for such luxury items in a micro region like Barkur it may be suggested that they had connections with the *Manigramam,* the trade guild of South India, which consisted of itinerant traders from different parts of South India.[11] At the same time we may suggest that the *manigaras* imported the precious stones and gems from other regions to export the same to those regions where these luxury goods were in great demand. The fact that Barkur was visited by several foreign traders like Arabs supports this suggestion. The importance of this street is indicated by the fact that it was situated in the heart of the town. In Murukeri or Mudukeri there existed three streets. This was a stronghold of businessmen called Settikaras. The existence of Nakharesvara temple here indicates the prominence of *Nakhara* guild in this *keri.*[12]

The name Arasikeri suggests that this *keri* must have been developed either by or in the name of some Queen.[13] Ranganakeri got its name from Ranganna Setti.[14] Vasantha Shetty wrote that the Hosakeri marked the completion of the *keri* system and the evolution of good system of municipal administration with ten *keris.*[15]

Barkur and Basrur had separate quarters for merchants dealing with different commodities. Though these merchants and trading settlements carried on their work peacefully in cordial atmosphere there were instances of mutual enmity and fight which often made the rulers interfere and settle the matters.[16]

Barkur, Basrur and Mangalore were the major trade centres. As early as 10th century there existed trade in Barkur. *Jamiu-T-Tawarikh* of Rashid-u-Din mentioned Fakanur as one of the cities on the Western coast. Fakanur is identified as Barkur. From this it may not be wrong to say that Barkur was a flourishing town in the tenth century and it was well known to the Muslim traders.[17] During the Vijayanagara times there was a tremendous increase in the commercial activity at Barkur. The port and the provincial capital was visited by foreign ships and ships from Malabar and they took cargoes of husked rice. Great stores of it were taken to Ormuz, Aden, Cannanore and Calicut and bartered for copper, coconut and molasses. Pepper was also exported from here. Merchants were engaged not only in export of articles produced locally, but also in the re-export of commodities which were imported from Ceylon and other countries. Articles like aloes and tabashir were also exported.[18]

Ibn Batuta who visited India during the early part of 14th century has left his account about trade in Barkur. He described Fakanur (Barkur) as a large town on an inlet and here he found a large quantity of sugar-canes which were unexcelled in the rest of India. The Chief of the Muslim community at Fakanur was called Basadaw. He possessed about thirty warships, commanded by a Muslim called Lula, who was an evildoer and a pirate and a robber of merchants. Ibn Batuta said: "When we anchored, the Sultan sent his son to us to stay on board the ship as a hostage. We went on shore to visit him and he treated us with utmost hospitality for three nights, as a mark of respect for the Sultan of India and also from a desire to make some profit by trading with the personnel of our vessels. It is a custom of theirs that every ship that passes by a town must needs anchor at it and give a present to the ruler.[19] This they call the "right of *bandar*". If anyone omits to do this, they sail out in pursuit of him, bring him into the port by force, double the tax on him, and prevent him proceeding on his journey as they wish."[20] Batuta also mentioned about the existence of sea pirates near Barkur.[21] The above description shows that the state took active interest in trade in Barkur and by 14th century Barkur had emerged as an important port town.

A copper plate inscription of A.D.1390 discovered in Humcha Jain *math* mentions the presence of outside traders in South Kanara. It states that when Ajasahu, son of Bhojasahu came to Barkur as a trader, he gave a gift probably to Parshwanatha *basadi* of Mudukeri. But Sahu was not a surname found in coastal Karnataka. In this inscription there is also reference to one Agarwal family. We know that Agarwal was not a surname that could be associated with South Kanara and it could be from North India.[22] This inscription gives a clue to the sea route of Ajasahu. He started his sea voyage from Malaya, passed through Kambhuja, crossed over the islands and finally landed in the coastal town of Barkur. He settled there after his long sea voyage. Further, the inscription enables us to know that two local people, Mahamuda and Marakala took interest in the sea voyage.[23]

Barkur during the course of time began to have connections with the upghat regions. Santara connections during 11th century A.D. and Tolaha activities here during 12th century A.D. contributed to the development of commercial contact with upghat regions. Expansion of Hoysala authority to Barkur and conversion of Barkur into a provincial capital of Vijayanagara empire went a long way in the growth of commercial contact with the upghat regions. The guilds which regulated the market to some extent in Barkur sent the goods imported from other countries to upghat regions and brought the goods of upghat regions to Barkur.[24] They carried on their business in various commodities. Inscriptional evidences from Barkur province show that there was import of bulls of good variety from above the ghats.[25] From this fact we may say that bullocks were imported into the coastal town of Basrur and other areas in South Kanara from above the Western Ghats. These bullocks were of good quality and were used in the transport of goods, that is, for pulling the bullock carts, in extracting sugar-cane juice and oil in the traditional mills, and also in ploughing the fields. This trade continued for a long period in the history of the region.[26]

Mangalore

The port of Mangalore was situated on the confluence of two rivers, Netravati and Gurupur. The structure of the river formed backwater, which increased the navigability of Mangalore port. Depth of the river allowed entry of unloaded ship near the port. The hinterland of port of Mangalore produced pepper, betelnut, coconut, sandalwood, cardamom and different varieties of rice.[27] From the beginning of Christian era Mangalore has been described in the indigenous as well as foreign literature as an important trade centre. According to a legend a Durga temple was built in the coastal town of Bappanad (Mulki), about 30 kilometres north of Mangalore. It looked like any other such temple but was unique in one sense.[28] It was built in A.D. 1168 by a prosperous Muslim trader and has since been open to both Muslims and Hindus. The town of Bappanad was named after Bappa Beary. Beary is the local word for a Muslim and it is derived from the word *vyavahari* which means trader.[29]

Many legends have gained currency regarding the construction of the temple at Bappanad. One of these is that Bappa, a trader from Kerala, was sailing north with his group when his 'dhow' floundered off the Bappanad coast. Goddess Durga appeared before him in a dream and said that his misfortune would end. The trader sailed northward and sold his merchandise at five times their price. The above legend shows that there existed trade relations between Kerala and South Kanara during the 12th century. From this it is also clear that the commercial significance of the settlement was due to the organised trading activities of the Muslim merchants of Arab and Turkish origins.[30]

The foreign traders who visited Mangalore gave a description of the trade in Mangalore. Ibn Batuta referred to Mangalore as Manjarur. According to him Mangalore was a large town on the inlet called ad-Dumb, which was the largest inlet on the Malabar coast. This town was visited by merchants from Fars and Yemen and they took pepper and ginger in large quantity. The Sultan of Mangalore was Rama Daw. Batuta further stated that there was a colony of about four thousand Muslims in Mangalore. They lived in a suburb alongside the town. Conflicts frequently broke out between Muslims and the townspeople. Nevertheless, the Sultan made peace between them because he needed merchants. Batuta observed that they refused to land until the Sultan sent his son. When they went to meet the Sultan they were treated with great consideration.[31] According to Duarte Barbosa in Mangalore there existed both Muslims and Hindus. Many ships took from Mangalore black rice which was better than the white one. The rice was taken to Malabar and it was quite cheap in Mangalore. Further Barbosa said that rice was taken in cargoes of Muslims to Aden. He stated that pepper available in Mangalore was of a higher quality.[32] Tom Pires described Mangalore as a port for ships and merchants, who traded with Cambay and with the kingdoms of Goa and Deccan and Ormuz, taking products of the country and bringing others. Further Pires says that there were garrisons in this port under a Captain. The king derived huge revenues from seaports.[33] The above references to Mangalore suggest that by 14th – 15th centuries Mangalore had emerged as an important trade centre where rice and pepper were available. This predominant position of Mangalore continued in the later period also.

The Italian traveller Pietro Della Valle gave a description of Mangalore. According to him, the port was in the mouth of two rivers, "one more Northern runs from the Lands of Banghel; the other more southern from those of Olala, which stands beyond the river southwards, or rather beyond the bay of saltwater, which is formed round and large, like a great Haven by the two rivers before their entrance into the Sea, whose flowing fills the same with the salt water. Mangalore stands between Olala and Banghel and in the middle of the bay right against the Mouth of the Harbor, into which the Fort extends itself, being almost encompassed with water on three sides. It is but small, the worst built of any I have seen in India, and, as the Captain told me one day... may rather be termed the House of a Gentleman than a Fort. The City is but little neither, contiguous to the Fort and encompassed with weak walls; within which the houses of inhabitants are enclosed. In Mangalore there are three churches..."[34]

The above description shows that the port was not well maintained. Thus when the enemies attacked the fort it was arduous task for the Portuguese to defend. Pietro Della Valle also mentioned the existence of market place (*bazaar*) in Banghel and Ullal,[35] where areca, cloth, gold knives and other merchandise were available for sale. In the interior regions, the merchants had to pay toll to the officials of Venkatappa Nayaka, the Keladi king.[36] Venkatappa Nayaka comprehended the importance of Portuguese for the economy of his kingdom. Pietro Della Valle states that Venkatappa Nayaka did not capture the Portuguese fort of Mangalore to "let those Portugals in that small place, in respect of the Traffick and Wares which they brought to the benefit of their countries".[37]

According to the English traveller Alexander Hamilton Mangalore was the premium port on the Kanara coast. He says "the Portuguese have a Factory for rice here, and a pretty large church, because great numbers of black Christians, reside there." Hamilton further says that, "the fields here bear two crops of corn yearly in the plains; and the higher grounds produce pepper, bettlenut, sandal wood, iron and steel, which make Mangulore a place of pretty good trade. The town is poorly built along the sides of the rivers, and has no defence against an enemy, but two small forts, one on each side of the river's mouth."[38] Here Hamilton repeated the statement of Pietro Della Valle that the town of Mangalore was not well defended. In 1695 the Arabs attacked and plundered Mangalore and carried a huge booty.[39] The trading community of Mangalore consisted of Muslims, Saraswats, Komatis, Virashaiva traders of Karnataka, Christians, Gujaratis, traders from Kerala and foreign traders belonging to Red Sea ports. According to the ***Livro do Cartazes,*** during the period from 1705 to 1724 8600 *khandis* were exported to different markets.[40] The destinations of Mangalore trade were Malabar, Goa, Surat, Bengal, Malacca, Maldives, Mecca, Aden, Congo, Hormuz and Ceylon.

Scholars like Meera Abraham have tried to discuss the role of South India in the international trade. It is said that fourteenth century was a time when finally a 'world system' came into being that integrated all five sections of old world trade: south west, south, south east, east Asia, plus the Mediterranean.[41] The ports of western coast of India had contacts with other ports of the world particularly the Arabian and Chinese. The Arab and Chinese traders used to visit the ports of both western and eastern coast. Thus when the Portuguese and other Europeans came to South India they did not do anything to seriously alter the already existing international trade but they only participated in it and augmented the volume of goods that were traded. Here we find continuity and further development in the international trade.

Our sources speak about the connections between the foreign traders and ports of the Western coast. Meera Abraham has analysed this kind of relations. It is said that in A.D.1282 the Chinese envoy arrived in Quilon. The Syrian Christian community in Quilon at that time still had trading interests. The head of the Christians accompanied the return mission from Quilon, as well as a representative of a neighbouring principality, perhaps Mangalore, another centre reputed for its fine pepper, as was Quilon.[42] This fact reveals the Chinese trade contacts with the Western coast of India and the interest of Chinese merchants in pepper trade.

The Yuan missions to Kollam on the west coast of India reveal interesting details relevant for our study. They indicate that there was a change in commodity demand and that new trade realities emerged which made the west coast of South India increasingly important commercially from the thirteenth century onwards. The west coast of India was drawn into more important trade relationships with West Asia and Egypt and through these regions with the European west. The trade between west coast of South India and Persian gulf, Yeminite coast and the Red Sea ports commenced much earlier, as found in the Islamic sources, but more precise information is available in the documents of the Cairo Geniza.[43]

Towards the end of twelfth century, European merchants were prohibited entry into the Red Sea. This protectionist move favoured the rapid development of the Egyptian corporate association of traders known as the Karimi. The main commodity of trade that the Karimi dealt in were pepper and spices. Pepper was sold to the Venetians at Alexandria.[44]

Two Judeo-Arabic documents on India trade (twelfth century) indicate that out of the four important ship owners, who were plying their ships between Mangalore and Aden, except perhaps one called Nambiyar, all others were Muslims.[45] The Jewish records on Indian trade reveal that merchant ships went from Mangalore to Aden via Diu on the coast of Saurashtra where local produce was collected.[46] This subject is also analysed by S.D. Goitein. The following details presented in his work are relevant in this context:[47]

"A representative of merchants in the capital of Egypt, stuck in Broach, north of Bombay, after having been captured by Pirates, is invited by his brother-in-law in Mangalore, to join him in his own ship on the way back to Aden. This document belonged to c. 1145. The writer of this letter, Mahruz ("protected by God") b. Jacob, was a *nakhoda*, or shipowner, who commuted in his own boat between Aden and India. Occasionally we find him in the capital of Egypt, where his sister was married to the recipient of this letter, Judah b.Joseph ha-Kohen, representative of the merchants there. Judah's own sister was married to Madmun, representative of the merchants in Aden. The letter says the following: In *(Your) Name O Merciful* "Your hand shall be lifted upon your adversaries, and all your enemies shall be cut off" I am writing to you.... I wish to inform you my lord, that I had previously written you at Tana. Meanwhile the accompanying boat of the ship arrived, and its soldiers told us that the ship in which your excellency my lord travelled was taken by pirates, and I was very sad about this. But afterwards I praised God and thanked him, when I heard that your life was saved. .... I would indeed like to mention my lord, that your servant had a large shipment in the boat of Fofali ("Betel-nut merchant"), then God ordained what happened (i.e. everything was lost).... Your servant thought that your honour my lord was in Tana, and I had previously sent letters to the *nakhoda* Tinbu, advising him to pay my lord 21 *mithqals* (Egyptian *dinars*) Afterwards, however, my lord the Sheikh Abu 'l-Qasim Ibn Qattan (dealer in cotton) came to Mangalore. I enquired about you and he told me that your excellency was in broach. In all circumstances, please come quickly to Mangalore and do not tarry, for I am waiting here in Mangalore and-if God wills-we shall embark on our way home as soon as possible. It is better for you to travel from Mangalore with me than to travel in the ships of foreign people. Please remember that there is no difference between us, my money is yours, it is just the same. The boats start presently from your place, from Kanbayat , and from Tana; please set out immediately so that you reach Mangalore with the vessels which, God willing, will soon be arriving in Malibarat(Malabar), Kayakannur and Mangalore. If my lord you need any gold, please take it on my account from the *nakhoda* Tinbu (a Hindu), for he is staying in Tana and between him and me there are bonds of inseparable friendship and brotherhood. You would certainly like to know, my lord, that a sum in favour of your excellency remained with me on account of the silk. With it I bought twelve and sixteen large [*bahars*] pepper for you, and I dispatch this for you under God's protection from Mangalore with the "Blessed"[48] ship-may God ordain her safety. Nor do I need to urge you again to come to Mangalore".

The above record gives information on merchants trading with betel nut and cotton at Mangalore. It throws light on the movement of ships from Aden to Mangalore. The foreign traders might have married native women. It is stated that Abraham Yiju married a slave girl Ashu in 1132 A.D.[49] Thus we may say that these Jewish traders bolstered their economic position by arranged family bonds.

The contemporary literature also reflects the presence of foreign traders and their influence on Indian culture. Ratnakaravarni's ***Bharatesha Vaibhava***, written during the 16th century, mentions Arabic, Parsee and Turkish words. For instance there is reference to words like *pauju* (Arabic, army), *gulama*(Arabic, slave), *nangalla*(Parsee, anchor), *teji*(Arabic, horse), *jambukhana*(Parsee, carpet) and *tupaki* (Turkish, rifle). Ratnakaravarni referred to Muslims as *gaddada turukaru* (bearded Turks). He referred to Ormuz as *Huramunzi*. In his work he also mentioned Mecca.[50] This shows that by 16th century the impact of foreign traders was well noticed in the society.

Folk version popular in Basrur region indicates that the Chinese merchants visited the coastal towns from Cranganore to Goa.[51] The accounts of Abdul Razzaq give us information about the existence of a considerable West Asian trading community at Vijayanagara and in the ports of the West coast which Vijayanagara kings always tried to control.[52]

The sources give information about the existence of Arab traders who later were indigenised and settled in Mangalore. The Muslim Mapillas belong to this category. The Arab sources indicate that the Arab traders were aware of the trade centres like Basrur, Barkur, Bekal, Kasaragod, Mangalore and Shirur. Yaqut said that from the Malabar region pepper was exported. According to him the famous cities of Malabar were Manjarur and Fakanur. Damishqui mentioned that Manibar adjoined Hunnur. It was also named as the country of pepper. There were many cities and the chief of them was Faknur.[53] Yaqut referred to the gulf of Fufal (identified with Bekal) while Damishqui said that the city of Fufal occupied a big area and that there were within it diving places for small pearls.[54]

Damishqui mentioned Harquilya (Kasaragod) which had a big area. It had under its control about one thousand villages, situated on hilly tracts as well as on the coast.[55] He also mentioned the city of Khurnal (Kumbla) which was a port for the ships of Hind as well as for those who passed by.[56] Damishqui and Abul Fida gave information about Manjarur

(Mangalore). Damishqui stated that the city of Manjarur was situated on a river known by the same name, and the river emptied into the sea where there was ebb and low tide. Large quantity of pepper was available here. Abul Fida stated that Manjarur was situated to the east of Sindabur, Hannur and Basrur. It is said that Manjarur is the biggest town in Manibar (Malabar).[57] Damishqui placed Saymur (Shirur) after Faknur in the list of cities of Malabar. According to him Saymur was on the coast, in a wide gulf through which big ships from the gulf of Faknur passed by, both the gulfs had ebb and low tide.[58]

Basrur

Basrur was an important trade centre. From middle of twelfth century the importance of Basrur was recognised, for, it was mentioned in an inscription dated 1155 A.D. It was known as Basurepura (town of Basrur) and also as Hosapattana (new town), indicating its new construction. In the middle of fifteenth century this town was known as Dharmapattan. From the middle of fourteenth century onwards, epigraphs refer to urban features of Basrur by mentioning different *keris* and settlements of different trading communities, namely, *halarus, settikaras, nakharas* and *hanjamanas.*[59] It is said that in Basrur there existed four doors to enter the town, two for those who went by road and two for those who went by river or water transport.[60] It is said that Basrur was actually a twin town. Mudukeri and Paduvakeri were two important *keris* which had certain resemblances. In both the *keris* there existed temples of Siva, Tirumala, Venkataramana and Ramachandra, *garadi* (gymnasium) and *agrahara* (Brahman settlement).[61]

Basrur consisted of various *keris* like Mandikeri, Vilasakeri, Ravutakeri, etc. *Mandi* was the place where wholesale trade of goods existed. In Mandikeri there was the arrival of traders and merchandise and there was facility to store goods in large pots. These *keris* had doors which were closed in the night and opened in the morning. In the Vilasakeri the traders used to relax with the help of perhaps prostitutes and other luxuries like intoxicating drinks, etc.[62]

The coastal towns had established connections with

upghat regions both due to commercial reasons as well as religious factors. The Hattiyangadi record speaks of the remission of half of the taxes on goods on the *nakhara* of Purigere. Both Purigere in Dharwad district and Hattiyangadi were great centres of Jainism. Being very close to the Arabian sea, and situated on the bank of the river Gangolli (Varahi), facing the famous port town of Basrur, Hattiyangadi might have attracted the Jain merchants of Purigere.[63]

Chara, now an ordinary village near Hebri in Karkal Taluk, was a flourishing commercial centre. This place is even today called *angadi-chara*. One of the inscriptions found in the same village states that two noble merchant brothers, Madanna Setti and Hosabu Setti, caused the construction of *chaityalaya* for Adinatha in A.D. 1432. The inscriptions refer to the existence of administrative bodies like *nadu* and *samasta halaru* and the merchant guilds such as *settikaras* and *nakharas*. This township might have played a significant commercial role as it was situated on the plains just below the Agumbe ghats, and very near to the sacred place of Varanga.[64]

Items of Trade

The chief articles of export from South Kanara were pepper, rice, coconuts, incense, perfumes, dyestuffs, sugarcane, *aloes, tabashis,* etc. The articles of import were Chinese silk, metals, pearls, sapphire, camphor, textiles, horses and even elephants. There were officers to regulate this trade and for the collection of tolls and taxes at ports and ferry points.

The above details indicate flourishing trade and commerce in South Kanara. This led to the emergence of trade guilds.

Trade and Transport

Trade in varieties of goods necessitated the existence of trade routes and a system of transport which facilitated transfer of goods from one region to the other. Trade also required the existence of currency even though the barter system was prevalent during this period. Because at the inter-regional and international level it was imperative for the traders to make use of currency. The Kings of Karnataka and the feudatory rulers issued coins of different denominations which were in circulation. In fact even at the all India level one can find the issue and use of large number of coins after 1000 A.D. During the earlier period flourishing trade did not exist. Therefore there was no much need for currency. But after 1000 A.D. the feudal practices declined and there was revival of trade. The emergence of Vijayanagara further facilitated the transition from feudalistic mode of production to pre-capitalist or proto-capitalist mode of production. This led to improvement in technology and the increase in the volume of trade. The arrival and presence of European traders like the Portuguese, Dutch and the English facilitated expansion of trade.

Land Transport

Some of the sources indicate the channels of trade. Mangalore had direct trade contacts with Banavara.[65] The inscriptions refer to Baraknur ghat, which passed through the western boundary of Hoysala Empire.[66] The Mangalore inscription belonging to Saka year 1311 mentions Harihararaya as the lord of east, west and southern seas.[67] This shows the realisation of the strategic importance of Western coastal regions. The coastal belt with many rivers and ports on the seacoast facilitated transfer of goods and trade, both coastal and overseas. By controlling the coastal ports it was possible to control the trade routes. Thus all rulers, native or foreign, aspired to control the districts of Western coastal regions since they were the gateways through which the goods were imported and exported. This inscription also mentions *voladari* (shorter route).[68] The inscriptions refer to ferry tolls and taxes on land routes. These revenue collections indicate that there existed river and road transport systems both in regional and inter-regional trade. Vijayanagara inscriptions from South Kanara allude to highways, roads, lands and footpaths (*raja-bidi, bidi, hiriya heddari, heddari, nadeva-oni,* etc.) The Basrur record of A.D. 1455 is significant in this regard.[69] According to this record the *halaru* of the Mudukeri of Basrur were obliged to set apart from the lands which they owned, a stretch of land measuring

12 *kolu* in breadth for purposes of laying a road for the use of local citizens as well as outsiders. Further it is stipulated that in the matter of carrying offerings to the temple of Devi, the above road was to be utilised only by the *halaru* of Mudukeri and not by *halaru* of Paduvakeri. The responsibility of relaying an old road of equal breadth in another part of Basrur devolved upon the *halaru* of Paduvakeri. On the sides of important roads, mango trees were grown for shade and shelter.[70] It is pointed out that *rajabidi* and *rajamarga* refer to main roads and the word *heddari* and *bidi* were also used to refer to the roads. *Oni* was a narrow path, which could not be used for taking carts. *Anchu* was a raised path between the paddy fields. Besides serving as a boundary between the two plots of land, it was helpful as a path for the people who carried things on head or took the goods on the back of animals.[71] There are references to the import of bullocks to South Kanara from the upghat region. They were sold in the periodic markets and fairs in Barkur and other regions. Commodities were brought from and taken to the up ghat regions by head loads and on bullocks.[72]

From the seventeenth century onwards some of the internal trade centres below the ghats were Bantwal, Bangadi, Belthangadi and Pane Mangalore. This is known from a record of 1642 A.D.[73] Kokkarne, Karkala, Someswara, Gersoppe were also prominent trade centres of varieties of agrarian products.[74] These were markets of agrarian and non-agrarian products such as grains, rice, paddy, arecanut, pepper and jaggery, oil, ghee, etc. Subsequently these towns became custom houses (*sunka thanes*)[75], where custom duties were collected. Subsequently many such towns were called *Sunkada Katte* in South Kanara.

Usually the agrarian products were carried on the back of the bullocks or carts drawn by bullocks. Ships and large boats were used for the sea trade. The roads in coastal region were fit for the movement of a large number of carts drawn by bullocks. The traders always moved in groups in these routes because they had to protect themselves from the attack of the robbers. It was always problematic for the traders to travel in the forests. The trade guilds hired the service of soldiers. The State also gave protection to the traders. This is supported by the accounts of foreign travellers. Ibn Batuta explains in detail the land route from Goa to Malabar. According to him it took two months along the coast to reach Quilon from Goa. The road over the whole distance ran beneath the shade of trees, and at every half mile there was a wooden shed with benches on which all travellers might sit. At each shed there was a well for drinking water and a person was in charge of them. He gave water to the travellers. At all halting places on this road there were houses belonging to Muslims, at which Muslim travellers alighted and bought all that they needed. No one travelled on an animal here and only the king possessed horses. The principal vehicle of inhabitants was a palanquin carried on the shoulders of slaves or hired porters. Those who did not travel on palanquins, travelled by foot. Hired carriers transported baggage and merchandise, and a single merchant might have a hundred or more of such carriers to carry his goods. Finally Ibn Batuta states that, "I have never seen a safer road than this, for they put to death anyone who steals a single nut, and if any fruit falls no one picks it up but the owner..."[76]

In 1516 Duarte Barbosa observed that the agrarian products such as rice, vegetables and sugar-cane produced in the interior regions were taken to coastal towns like Baindur, Basrur, Mangalore and Kumbla by means of *kavades*[77], on head loads, pack horses, pack bullock carts and asses.[78] Barbosa stated that in *Tulunadu* there were many rivers and towns where there was much seafaring and traffic in goods of different kinds. He noted the transportation of goods in small *zambuquos*.[79] In 1522 Domingo Paes also observed that the roads which connected Vijaynagara with Goa, Bankapur, Banavasi, Honnavar and Bhatkal were fit for the transport of agrarian products by means of carts and bullocks. From these roads agrarian products passed from one region to the other.[80] In 1623 A.D. there were roads that connected Ikkeri, Sagar and other interior towns.[81] Pietro Della Valle said that the highways of Venkatappa Nayaka's country were very secure. Further describing the roads, he said, "the roads lay over pleasant peaks of hills and through woods, many great streams likewise occuring".[82] Della Valle described an incident, which occurred in Basrur coast where there was the danger of their ships being broken when one ship hit a rock in the sea. The narration of this incident indicates that there were many problems for the traders on sea.[83] While travelling to Mangalore Della Valle stayed in a rest house, owned by a brahman, called *Bamanen coppa*(Brahman's grove).The distance was described in terms of *gaus, kos* and leagues. One *gau* was equal to two *kos* and two Portuguese leagues. Della Valle travelled on his horse accompanied by a *pulia* (untouchable, lowest in the Indian social hierarchy) who carried the luggage on his back.[84] According to an English traveller, Fryer, the roads in coastal Karnataka were broad, not in the bypass as in the nation called the Malabars.[85] The prominent ports in South Kanara were connected with hinterland by plain roads with four rows of trees.[86] According to Alexander Hamilton the road from Basrur to Mangalore consisted of four rows of trees which made journey comfortable since the plants provided shelter to travellers. He says that there were huts built, where some old people stayed in the daytime with jars of fine clear water for the passenger to drink at the charge of the state. Barkur and Mulki lied between Basrur and Mangalore. Both Mangalore and Basrur enjoyed the benefit of rivers to export the large quantities of rice that their fields produced. Further Hamilton stated that Mangalore was the greatest mart for trade in Kanara. It had the convenience of one river, which was connected by three other rivers from north, south and east. These rivers proceeded from the great rains and dews that fell from the mountains. These three rivers joined about a mile from the sea and at Mangalore formed a common receptor of rivers.[87] The roads were used for transporting the agrarian products from hinterland to the ports. The roads which connected Bednur with the seaports in the reign of Keladi Basavappa Nayaka II (1739-1756 A.D.) were very fine planted with trees and safe and no stranger was ever robbed or molested there.[88] On such roads large number of bullock carts laden with the agrarian products such as rice, paddy, arecanut, coconut, ragi, jowar, oil seeds, etc., used to travel from above and below the Sahyadri region as mentioned in inscriptions.[89] Linschoten noted the distance between Honnavar, Basrur and Mangalore towns as follows:[90]

Honnavar————— Basrur—— 15 miles

Basrur——————Mangalore—9 Miles

However, he failed to record them correctly.

Boats, large and small ships and rafts were used for coastal and sea trade. The rivers in South Kanara facilitated inland traffic. These rivers were relatively more wider, deeper and more navigable as they approached the Sea. The Portuguese sources refer to different types of local vessels. But it is difficult to determine their size, capacity and mast. There were boats with oars and sails. The local traders had their own vessels manned by the local people like Mogers, Karvis, Mukkavars, Mapillas, etc. The Portuguese records inform about the boats that left from Kanara to Goa. The native ships carried rice, pepper and coconut to Malabar, Arabia and Red Sea region.[91] In the beginning of the seventeenth century, Francois Pyrard noticed the vessels, owned by the Kanarese in the Maldive islands.[92] A few Kannada letters belonging to the second half of eighteenth century kept in the Cochin archives state that huge ships and rafts owned by the natives of Mangalore used to carry coconut and rice to the ports in Malabar and coastal Karnataka.[93] Muslims and the low caste Hindus manned the ships and the boats, which used to carry the agrarian products, though their owners and financiers were likely to be the local high caste Hindus.[94] In the eighteenth century, ports of Kumbla, Manjeshwar and Mangalore had contacts with the Western ghat region by means of roads. Several bullock carts carrying coconut, arecanut, sugar, ragi, jowar, rice, jaggery, etc. used to pass daily on these roads to the above ports.[95] The Keladi chiefs levied taxes on the goods passing through the roads known as *rahadari sunka*.[96] During the time of Basavappa Nayaka the roads were connected with the seaport.[97] Sometimes the roads were not well maintained.

The communication between the district and the country above the ghats was maintained by means of seven well traced roads through passes in the Western ghats, besides a number of paths and cattle tracks. The main roads from five out of seven passes converged at Mangalore. These passes were at Sampaje ghat, Shiradi ghat, Bisli ghat and Charmadi ghat. The next pass was at Agumbe to the north of the Udupi taluk, and near Someshwar at the foot of the pass, roads branched off towards the ports of Kundapur, Barkur and Udupi, but the main road went on to Mangalore. The Hosangadi ghat from Bednore or Nagar had direct communication only with the river which led to the port of Kundapur, to which port also came the road from Kollur pass. The number of broad estuaries and backwaters and the long stretches of sand near the coast made it impossible to have a thoroughly satisfactory coast road.[98] The above details indicate that South Kanara was connected with different parts of Karnataka and South India during the pre-modern period. The transportation of goods particularly in the Western ghats, was relatively slower, difficult and it took several days to reach a destination.

River Traffic

There was a strong tradition of shipbuilding in Kanara. Medium sized craft was used in the coastal trade of Western India. The shipbuilding centres had better access to high quality timber in hinterland forests. The rulers and merchants strongly supported shipbuilding activities.[99] As seen earlier it was one of the industrial activities which thrived in the region. Certain boats were common in the West coast. For instance, the *manche* (a small craft) was found all over the Malabar Coast up to Kanara.[100]

The Kanara coast consisted of numerous creeks and bays formed by the estuaries of rivers. These rivers ran from east to west and flowed into the Arabian Sea. All the rivers did not facilitate easy traffic. The Kundapur River was only navigable by boats and small vessels. Large ships could not approach the shore here. The Netravati river near Mangalore was navigable for boats for many miles up to Bantwal. The bar had only 6 or 7 feet on it at low spring tides so that only small vessels could enter. Arab vessels of 150 tons managed to get in at high springs but the larger ships, which brought horses from the Persian Gulf were compelled to lie out in the roadstead.[101] Della Valle described the travel by boat. In Mangalore he engaged a boat in which there were three water men, two of whom rowed at the prow and one at the poop, with a broad oar which served both for an oar and a helm.[102]

L.N. Swamy and G.V.Rajamanickam have classified the boats into five major categories, such as *teppa, harigolu, doni, nave* and *hadagu.* The first two categories were not seaworthy crafts where as the next three were seaworthy. The first two categories were used for river transportation. The above five categories were sometimes classified into four major groups, namely, rafts, skin boats, log boats and plank built boats. The *teppa* and *harigolu* came under rafts and skin boats respectively. Crafts that came under *doni* variety denoted log boats. *Nave* and *hadagu* came under the plank built boat class. The rivers of South India were not easily navigable. Hence boats and rafts were used only to cross the rivers wherever the bridges were not constructed. *Harigolu* was used only in inland transportation mainly for the purpose of crossing the rivers, fishing and to overcome the whirlpools, which were common in the rivers.[103]

Studies on the Portuguese commercial activities in Kanara have shown that porters and pack animals like horses, bullocks and asses were the usual means of transport on land. Boats and ships were the most important means of water transport. *Empalega catacoulo* and *calamute* were the smallest of local vessels. Larger than these were *parao, manchua, sanguicel, pinnace, cathia, gundra, taurim, paquel* and *zambuco.* There were also large *taurim* and large *paquel* and *nau,* which were the largest local ships. These were the vessels, which were common on the coasts of coastal Karnataka as well as Malabar in the sixteenth century.[104] Eighteenth century records mention that the *machwas, manchi, grubs, hai padagu* and *hai doni* arrived from Arabia and Kochi to the port of Mangalore.[105] It is mentioned that a record of eighteenth century mentions vessels such as *almadia* (an Arabic word for large raft, but generally used for Indian canoe), *caravel* (a vessel of about 200 tons known for its speed), *pattamara* (a rigged ship with one or three masts), *paranguee* (a kind of cargo boat, perhaps an European ship) and *gallivat* (a boat having oars and triangular sail).[106] Earlier the local ships did not have any provision for weapons to protect themselves from the attack of the enemies or sea pirates. But it was the Portuguese who introduced the system of the merchant ships carrying guns and gun powder to fight against the pirates and enemies. There were also fleets of military ships which protected the merchant ships on the sea.

The folklore of South Kanara furnish some details about river transport system. In the *Jarandaya paddana* it is mentioned that Jarandaya came to the Atrel ferry. He ordered the ferryman, Kunya, to bring the ferryboat. But the ferryman said that the boat did not belong to him and that he was not supposed to get the fare. Further he revealed that one Kote Bale Bermane had kept the boat for crossing the river on Tuesdays and Sundays Then Jarandaya said, "No matter if the boat is kept by him for crossing the river; I will give you the proper fare, Bring the boat to this side" As soon as he had said this, the ferryman brought the boat.[107] The ferry owners controlled large villages and sometimes even a town. There were definite days for ferrying persons across rivers.[108]

The folklore mention loads carried by man who acted as beast of burden. The most popular vehicle carried on man's shoulder was a sort of hammock called in Tulu

Mancil.[109] The rivers had sometimes bridges of ropes built over them. On their way to Edamburu, Koti and Chennaya crossed a bridge of ropes.[110] The rest houses on the roads gave shelter to travellers. Koti and Chennaya were given food and water by a brahman keeper of such a rest house. These rest houses were called *kattes.* There were three different kinds of drinking cups- one for giving water to aristocrats and princes, another a smaller one for brahmans and third one of a bell-metal for people of all castes.[111] The beasts of burden used in early times were the elephants, the horse, the ox and the camel. The Perimale Ballala presented Sama Alva with a camel to carry the heavy load of liquor home.[112]

Pirates

One danger that the traders had to encounter on the sea was that of sea pirates among whom the Mapillas were well known. In one such incident, which took place near Mangalore, they resorted to confiscation of ships and their cargoes. Therefore the ships which sailed there in summer laid in their cargoes in six or eight days and departed from there as fast as possible.[113] Ibn Batuta described one incident in which pirates with twelve war ships attacked him and his associates and they plundered the goods. These goods consisted of jewels, precious stones, clothes, and provisions.[114] The Portuguese were also afraid of pirates. At Kumbla the Portuguese discovered twelve ships coming towards them as though from the south, which need not be necessarily from Malabar. They judged them to be "paroes" as indeed they appeared to be, but they were almost like ships of Portugal but somewhat lighter. The Portuguese prepared to fight them and, sailing forward to meet them, found them an unexpected and extraordinary fleet of the Portuguese sent to the Konkan.[115]

Markets

There were weekly markets (*santhes*) and fairs (*jatres*). Weekly markets were held on certain fixed days once a week in almost every village. In these markets interaction between the seller and buyer was direct without the intervention of the middlemen. The peasant and the craftsmen took their produce from permanent warehouses or shops to temporary market places. Barter system coexisted with cash dealings. In places where periodical markets were rare, people procured articles of consumption from small bazars where petty traders sold them by retail. The goods that were traded in these markets included agricultural produce of all kinds, coarse and superfine cloth, salt, timber, iron utensils, baskets, etc. Fairs or *jatres* were held usually during certain religious festivals. At these fairs the articles traded were common-use provisions, knives, scissors and glasses, cattle and sheep. It was an occasion for the exchange of the products of distant places. In South Kanara, major fairs were held at the time of festivals of Subrahmanya, Dharmasthala, Udupi and Kollur. The approximate number of people who attended these fairs during 18th century were as below:[116]

Name of Jatre	*Number of People Attended*
Subrahmanya	30,000
Dharmasthala	10,000
Udupi Paryaya	12,000
Kollur car festival	15,000

The people attended these festivals with a view to attain religious merit, the traders established their shops in these places and they benefited by the religious festivals by selling their goods to the pilgrims.[117]

The *Hamsavimshati,* a work of eighteenth century gives a list of places, where merchants gathered for the sale and purchase of commodities. It mentions Udupi.[118] It is quite probable that the traders from these market places were visiting South Kanara.

Currency

According to the feudalism theory applied in the case of India, after 5th century there was lack of coins and there was decline of trade which led to de-urbanisation.[119] However, after 11th century again there was revival of trade and we find references to coins in the sources. Even in the case of South Kanara after 12th century we find references to different types of currency, which indicate increased monetisation of the economy. According to B.A.Saletore by the first quarter of the 12th century A.D. South Kanara had adopted the monetary system of other parts of Karnataka.[120] During the Vijayanagara period, there were increased contacts with the foreign traders, particularly with the Arabs and the Portuguese. As a result of this we find that after 14th century the sources speak about the use of foreign coins in South Kanara.

The sources indicate that there were different types of currency in circulation. The Alupa inscriptions mention some of the coins. The Panchalingeswara temple inscription of Kavi Alupendra refers to coin *Pandya gadyana*.[121] It is also mentioned as *honnu,* which suggests that this was a gold coin.[122] According to K. V. Ramesh, the Pandyas of South India issued these coins and they were die-struck. He further says that the name *gadyana* was applied to coins struck from more than one metal because in the inscriptions there are specific references to *honna gadyana* or gold coin.[123] With the marked increase in commerce money came into wider circulation. While during the pre 11th century period taxes were paid in kind, after 12th century we find references to taxes being paid in money. The most common types of coins in circulation were known as *gadyana, varaha, honnu* and *hana*. We also find reference to different other denominations like *kati-gadyana, ardha-kati gadyana* and *bahira gadyana.* The latter seems to be a foreign coin struck outside South Kanara and brought into circulation in the region.[124] According to A.V.Narasimha Murthy among the coins issued by the Vijayanagara kings, the majority were of gold. According to some foreign travellers the coins were not pure but according to some inscriptions the purity was 80 to 90%. The coins of the Vijaynagara period were *gadyana, varaha, pon, pagoda, pratapa, kati, pana, chinna, mada, haga, visa, bele, ruka* and *kasu.* The value and the weight of each of these coins are given as follows:[125]

Gold Coins

dodda varaha=dodda gadyana =2 *varaha* = 120 grain

1 *gadyana* = 1 *varaha* = 1 *pon* = 1 *pagoda* =52 grain

1 *varaha* = 2 *pratapa* = 1 *mada* = 52 grain

1 *pratapa* = 2 *kati* = 26 grain = ½ *varaha*

1 *kati* = 13 grain = ¼ *varaha*

1 *varaha* = 10 *pana* = 5-6 grain

1 *chinna* = 6.5 grain = 1/8 *varaha*

1 *pana* = 4 *haga* = 5-6 grain

1 *haga* = 2 *bele* = 1.5 grain

Silver Coins

Tar =1/6 *pana*

Tara = 1/16 *pana*

Copper Coins

Duggani = 2 *kani* or 2 *kakini* = 250 grain

1 *kani* = 125 grain = 2 *arekani*

1 *jital* = 1/3 *tara*

1 *kasu* = 30 grain

1 *arekasu* = 15 grain

A copper plate inscription belonging to Saka year 1509 mentions the value of coins as follows:[126]

Varaha = 4 Rupees

Honnu= ½ *varaha*

Hana = 1/10 *varaha*

Haga = ¼ *hana*

The above details indicate that during the Vijaynagara period there was the standardisation of the monetary value of the different types of coins. This went a long way in systematising the currency system.

The introduction of coined money on a large scale revolutionised the entire economy of the Kanara coast. The retail business was probably done entirely on money exchange. Even the village revenues were fixed on coined-money rates and it was called *samudaya gadyana*.[127] The inscriptions refer to *Barakura-gadyana* and *Mangalura-gadyana*. K. V. Ramesh suggests that these two names might have denoted coins issued from the royal mints at Barkur and Mangalore, the two capital cities of medieval Alupas.[128] B. Vasantha Shetty and K. G. Vasanthamadhava agreed with the above view. According to A.V. Narasimha Murthy the Vijayanagara king Harihara established a new office to look after the work of the minting of coins throughout the empire. Mint houses were established in Barkur and Mangalore and many other regions. There remained regional differences between the weight and the value of coins that were minted in different regions ruled by different Governors. This created confusion among the foreign traders as mentioned in the accounts of Caesar Fredrick. But this confusion might have existed only in the case of copper coins and not in the case of gold and silver coins since the gold and silver coins issued by the Vijaynagara kings were accepted throughout the empire. The officers in the mint houses were given the responsibility of maintaining the purity and the weight of the coins. The goldsmiths, who always accompanied the instruments necessary to test the quality of coins, assisted them. Thus the state was able to standardise the monetary system with the heip of the mint officers. The mint houses also acted as the agent of state by accepting the money that the people of the locality gave to the state as taxes and other dues. The moneylenders and the bankers also employed goldsmiths to test the quality of the coins.[129] Those traders who came to trade with South Kanara had to exchange their coins with the coins of Barkur mint house.[130]

Some inscriptions have mentioned the value of the coins. For instance, Kambhadakone (Kallutodame) inscription of A.D. 1561 mentions that 30 *varaha gadyana* was equal to 50 *katigadyana* and 60 *varaha gadyana* was equal to 100 *katigadyana*.[131] During the Vijaynagara period there are references to different categories of *gadyanas* like *dodda varaha gadyana*[132] *(nija gadyana), varaha gadyana, kodanda gadyana*[133] and *kathari ankusha gadyana*[134]. Both *gadyana* and *varaha* were used in the payment of taxes to the state, purchase and sale of land, donations to the temples for religious purposes. But after 16th century *gadyana* lost its importance and transactions were done in *varahas.*[135] Even then there was no major difference between the weight and the value of *varaha* and *gadyana.* Hence we may not attach too much importance to the replacement of *gadyana* by *varaha.*

The Jain merchant guilds seem to have organised financial institutions for mutual benefit and for the benefit of the king and the people. The individual merchants came forward to receive the gifted temple-money as loan for which amount they paid regularly a stipulated sum of money as interest. This was done either at the will of the merchants or at the instance of the temple authorities.[136] Initially the rate of interest was given in kind. The Basrur inscription mentions that for 200 *katigadyana* 13 *mude* rice was the rate of interest.[137] Later the rate of interest was given in the form of money. The Barkur inscription of A.D. 1499[138] mentions that for 300 *varaha gadyana* the rate of interest was 30 *dodda varaha gadyana*. An inscription belonging to A.D. 1548[139] mentions that for 50*varaha gadyana,* 5 *varaha gadyana* was the rate of interest. Thus it may be said that there existed the practice of lending loans and charging a fixed rate of interest. This is particularly plausible in the case of merchants who participated in the long distance trade and according to the profits in trade rate of interest also might have varied. For instance this practice was found in the banking of ancient India. Long distance trade meant greater risk factor and greater profit since the traders who participated in long distance trade usually traded in luxury items.

Systematic minting of coins was continued during the period of the Keladi kings. *Ikkeri varaha* was a gold coin which was minted in Nagara. The state gave the contract of minting the coins to certain individuals in Bhatkal and other regions. The coins that were in use during this period were *varaha, honnu, dharana, hana, mupaga, adda, haga, bele, visa* and *arevisa.*[140]

A few coins of foreign origin were discovered in South Kanara. A few Ceylonese coins were found in Mangalore. These coins bear the names of Rani Leelavati, Vijayabahu and Sasmalla and these were assigned to the 10th century A.D. These Ceylonese coins represent the Chola currency. Other foreign coins like *dinar* of Egypt and *ducat* of Venice and Florence were exchanged with the native coins of *pagoda* or *varaha*. The exchange value of these foreign coins was nearly equal to the indigenous coins. The Portuguese issued different denominations of coins and used in their trade transactions in rice and pepper with the local merchants. They issued coins like *xerafins, sao-tomes, cuzados* and *reis.* Afonso de Albuquerque issued coins equivalent to local ones. The Portuguese coins had the same value as the native ones. A *pardao (pratapa)* was equal to 320 *reis.* At the same time, the Portuguese traders used the native coins for their transactions in agricultural products. For them the native gold coin in South Kanara was *pagoda.* In 1630 the value of 102 *sao-tomes* was equal to 100 *pagodas* of Ikkeri.[141] Thus from the 10th century A.D. onwards there was development in the system of coinage in South

Kanara and with the emergence of Vijaynagara and Keladi kingdoms and the arrival of Portuguese and the English traders there was greater monetisation of the economy. There was great increase in the import of bullion into South Kanara and the traders became more prosperous. This development helped in the greater stabilisation of the economy of the region.

Notes and References

1. ***Indian Antiquary*** XVI, P. 31.
2. B Vasantha Shetty, **"Barakuru-A Metropolitan City of Antiquity"**, *Op. Cit*, PP. 103-106.
3. B. Vasantha Shetty, *Ibid*, P.295.
4. P. N. Narasimha Murthy, *Op. Cit.*, 1983, P. 472.
5. B. Vasantha Shetty , *Op. Cit.*, P. 268.
6. ***SII***, Vol. VII, No. 376.
7. B. Vasantha Shetty, *Op. Cit.*, P. 271.
8. *Ibid*, P. 273.
9. *Ibid*, P. 274. They were prominent in other urban centres like Basrur, where a merchant belonging to Balegara community made a land grant to a *math*. See ***SII***, Vol. IX Part II, No.446.
10. B. Vasantha Shetty,*Op. Cit.*, P. 276.
11. R. Champakalakshmi ,*Op.Cit.*, PP. 48-49 ; Meera Abraham, *Op. Cit*, PP. 14-39.
12. B. Vasantha Shetty, *Op. Cit.*, PP 275-276.
13. *Ibid*, P. 278.
14. *Ibid*, P. 279.
15. *Ibid*, P. 280.
16. P. N. Narasimha Murthy, *Op. Cit.*, 1983, PP 471-2.
17. *Ibid*, P.313.
18. *Ibid*, P. 314.

19. This system can be compared with the Portuguese system of issuing *cartazes* or passports to merchant ships and they were given protection by the Portuguese armada and those did not take Portuguese *cartazes* were attacked and as a result frequent conflicts arose between the Portuguese and the Muslim sea pirates on the western coast.

20. H. A. R. Gibb (Tr.), ***Ibn Batuta Travels in Asia and Africa 1324-1354***, *Op. Cit*, PP. 233-234.

21. *Ibid*, P. 265.

22. B. Vasantha Shetty, *Op. Cit.*, P. 319.

23. K. G. Vasathamadhava, 'A Review of indigenous sources of Trans-oceanic Activities of Coastal Karnataka A.D. 1000-1800', S.R. Rao (Ed.), ***An Integrated Approach to Marine Archaeology***, *Op. Cit,* P. 121.

24. B Vasantha Shetty, *Op. Cit.,* P. 320.

25. *Ibid*, P. 321.

26. Its importance dwindled in the twentieth century because of development of the modern means of transport, use of machinery in tilling the land and decline of sugar and jaggery industries.

27. K.G. Vasanthamadhava, ***Western Karnataka Its Agrarian Relations 1500-1800,*** New Delhi, 1991, P. 242.

28. ***E.C.,***VII, Sravanabelagola, 465-466.

29. Bappanad is a famous religious centre today also.

30. Om Prakash Prasad, ' Towns in early medieval Karnataka' in Vijay K. Thakur, ***Towns in Pre-modern India,*** *Op. Cit*, PP. 173-174.

31. H.A.R. Gibb (Translated and Selected) ***Ibn Batuta Travels in Asia and Africa 1325-1354,*** *Op. Cit.,* PP. 233-234.

32. Mansel Longworth Dames (Ed.), ***The Book of Duarte Barbosa,*** *Op. Cit.,* PP. 195-196.

33. Armando Cortesao (Ed.), ***The Suma Oriental of Tom Pires,*** Vol. I, New Delhi, 1990, PP. 60-63

34. Edward Gray(Ed.), ***The Travels of Pietro Della Valle in India***, Vol. II, New Delhi, 1991, P. 301.

35. ***Ibid,*** PP. 302-303.

36. ***Ibid,*** PP. 304-306.

37. ***Ibid,*** PP. 314-315.

38. Alexander Hamilton, ***A New Account of the East Indies 1688-1723,*** Vol. I, London, 1739, Madras, 1995, PP. 282-283.

39. ***Ibid,*** P. 283.

40. ***Livro do Cartazes, Historical Archives, Goa,*** MS. No. 1363.

41. *Ibid,* P. 9.

42. Meera Abraham, ***Two Medieval Merchant Guilds of South India***, *Op. Cit*, P. 150.

43. S.D.Goitien, 'Letters and Documents on the India Trade in Medieval Times', ***Islamic Cultue***, 37, January, 1963, P. 196, quoted in Meera Abraham, *Op. Cit.,* P.151.

44. W. J. Fischel, 'The Spice Trade in Mamluk Egypt, A Contribution to the Economic History of Medieval Islam', *JESHO*, 1, (1958), P. 160 quoted in Meera Abraham, *Op. Cit.,* P. 152.

45. S. D. Gotien, 'From Aden to India', *JESHO*, XXIII, 1980, P. 43 quoted in V. K. Jain, ***Trade and Traders in Western India (A.D.1000-1300)***, *Op. Cit*, P. 82.

46. V. K. Jain, *Op. Cit.,* P. 125.

47. S.D. Goitein, ***Letters of Medieval Jewish Traders,****Op. Cit*, PP. 62-65.

48. The "Blessed" (ship) belonged to Madmun of Aden and operated between Aden and Mangalore, ***India Book***, 28 V, II, 5-6, quoted in S.D. Goitien, ***Letters of Medieval Jewish Traders*** *Op. Cit.* P. 65.

49. *Ibid,* P. 202.

50. Heranje Krishna Bhatta (Ed.), ***Govinda Pai Samshodhana Samputa***, *Op. Cit,* P. 428.

51. K. G. Vasanthamadhava, 'Urban features of Gove under the Vijayanagara rule 1336-1472 A.D.' Unpublished paper, P. 4.

52. Sanjay Subrahmanyam, ***Vasco da Gama***, Cambridge University Press, 1997, P. 100.

53. S. Muhammad Husayn Nainar (Ed.), ***The Knowledge of India Possessed by Arab Geographers Down to the 14th Century A.D. with Special Reference to Southern India,****Op. Cit*, PP. 33-

34. The Arab travellers were under the impression that Kanara was the part of Malabar and therefore they mentioned that Mangalore and Barkur were important trade centres of Malabar.

54. *Ibid,* P. 37.

55. *Ibid*, P. 39.

56. *Ibid*, P. 50.

57. *Ibid*, P. 61.

58. *Ibid,* PP. 71-72.

59. K. G.Vasanthamadhava, ***Trends in Karnataka Historical Research,*** *Op. Cit.,* P. 95.

60. B. Lakshminarayana Upadhya, ' Pravasigara Tana Basaruru Nagara Noda Banni' in *idem* (Ed.), ***Hesarada Pattana asaruru Ondu Adhyayana***(in Kannada), Basrur, 1997, P.10.

61. *Ibid.*

62. *Ibid,* P. 11

63. P. N. Narasimha Murthy, *Op. Cit.,* PP. 473-4.

64. *Ibid,* PP 478-79.

65. Om Prakash Prasad, ***Decay and Revival of Urban Centres in Medieval South India***, *Op. Cit.,* P. 86.

66. ***Indian Antiquary***, Vol. XVI, P. 31.

67. ***S.I.I.*** Vol. VII, No. 190.

68. *Ibid.*

69. *Ibid*, Vol. IX, Part II, No. 457.

70. K. V. Ramesh, ***A History of South Kanara***, *Op. Cit.,* P. 281.

71. B. Vasantha Shetty, **"Barkur - A Metropolitan City of Antiquity'**, *Op. Cit.,* P. 324.

72. *Ibid*, PP. 321-323.

73. Ganapati Rao Aigal, ***Dakshina Kannada Jilleya Prachina Itihasa***, *Op. Cit.,* P. 438.

74. *Ibid*, Appendix No. 14; ***E.C.,*** VII, Shikaripur, No. 28.

75. K. G. Vasanthamadhava, ***Western Karnataka Its Agrarian Relations 1500-1800,*** *Op. Cit.*, P. 144.

76. H. A. R. Gibb (Tr.), ***Travels in Asia and Africa 1325-1354,*** *Op. Cit.*, PP. 231-232.

77. *Kavades* meant big sticks taking loads hanging on each side and it was carried on shoulder.

78. Mansel Longworth Dames (Ed.), ***The Book of Duarte Barbosa***, *Op. Cit,* P. 181 and P. 197.

79. *Ibid*, PP. 182-184.

80. Robert Sewell, ***A Forgotten Empire Vijayanagara***, New Delhi, 1962, P. 119.

81. Edward Gray (Ed.), ***The Travels of Pietro Della Valle, Vol.II***, *Op. Cit*, P. 266.

82. *Ibid*, P. 294.

83. *Ibid*, PP. 299-300.

84. *Ibid,* PP. 294-297.

85. John Fryer's account of India published in ***Calcutta Weekly English Man,*** London, 1873, P.224.

86. Alexander Hamilton, ***A New Account of the East Indies 1688-1723, Vol. I***, *Op. Cit,* P. 159.

87. *Ibid,* PP. 281-282.

88. Lewis Rice, ***Mysore and Coorg from Inscriptions, II,*** London, 1909, P. 435.

89. ***E.C.***, VIII, Tirthahalli, Nos. 83, 92, 68, 69.

90. Arthur Coke Burnell (Ed.), ***The Voyage of John Huyghen Van Linschoten to the East Indies***, *Op. Cit*, PP. 66-67.

91. M.N.Pearson, ***Coastal Western India***, *Op. Cit*, P. 77, P. 123 and P. 125.

92. Edward Gray (Tr. & Ed.), ***The Voyage of Francois Pyrard of Laval***, two volumes, Haklyut, 1887-90, quoted in K.G. Vasanthamadhava, ***Western Karnataka Its Agrarian Relations,*** *Op. Cit.*, P. 147.

93. K. G. Vasanthamadhava, ' A Note on Kannada paper in Cochin Archives', ***Indian Archives***, XXVII, 1978, No. 2, PP. 33-36.

94. K. G. Vasanthamadhava, ***Western Karnataka Its Agrarian Relations***, *Op. Cit*, P. 148.

95. K. G. Vasanthamadhava, 'Sea-faring Activities in the coastal Karnataka in the Eighteenth century', ***Eighteenth Century India***, Trivandrum, 1981, PP. 210-11.

96. Ganapati Rao Aigal, ***Dakshina Kannada Jilleya Pracina Itihasa***, *Op. Cit.*, Appendix Nos. 14, 15.

97. B. L. Rice, ***Mysore and Coorg from Inscriptions, II***, *Op. Cit.*, P.435.

98. Sturrock, , *Op. Cit*, PP. 14-15.

99. S. Arasaratnam, ***Maritime India in the Seventeenth Century***, Delhi, 1994, P. 255.

100. *Ibid*, P. 260.

101. John Sturrock, *Op. Cit.*, PP. 3-8.

102. Edward Gray (Ed.), ***The Travels of Pietro Della Valle, Vol.II***, *Op.Cit.*, P. 305.

103. L. N. Swamy and Rajamanickam G.V., 'Ships and boats as gleaned from Kannada literature', S.R:Rao (Ed.), ***An Integrated Approach to Marine Archaeology***, *Op. Cit*, PP. 59-60.

104. B.S.Shastry, 'Commercial Policy of the Portuguese in Coastal Karnataka: Sixteenth Century', H. V. Shrinivasamurthy *et.al.* (Eds.), ***Essays on Indian History and Culture***, *Op. Cit*, P. 119.

105. K.G.Vasanthamadhava, 'A Review of Indigenous sources of Trans-oceanic Activities of Coastal Karnataka A.D. 1000-1800' S.R.Rao(Ed.), ***An Integrated Approach to Marine Archaeology***, *Op. Cit*, P. 122.

106. K. G. Vasanthamadhava, 'Sea trade in the Ports of Kasargod', unpublished research paper presented in International Conference on Marine Archaeology, Thana, 1998, P.3.

107. ***Indian Antiquary***, Vol. XXIII, PP. 8-9.

108. B. A. Saletore, ***Ancient Karnataka, Vol. I, History of Tuluva***, *Op. Cit.*, P. 517.

109. ***Indian Antiquary,*** XXIII, P. 82.

110. B. A. Saletore, *Op. Cit.*, P. 519.

111. *Ibid*, P. 521

112. *Ibid*, PP. 522-523.

113. R. N. Saletore, ***Indian Pirates***, Delhi, 1978, P. 30.

114. H. A. R. Gibb (Tr.)***Ibn Batuta Travels in Asia and Africa 1325-1354***, *Op. Cit.,* P. 265.

115. *Ibid*, PP. 59-60.

116. Malathi K Moorthy, "**Trade and Commerce in Colonial South Kanara (1799-1862)**", *Op. Cit*, PP. 104-107.

117. For a folklorist study of the fairs, see Chandrashekhara Damle, ***Jatregala Ondu Janapadiya Adhyayana***, (in Kannada), Udupi, 1995.

118. N. Venkataramanayya , ***Studies in the History of Third Dynasty of Vijayanagara***, Delhi, 1986, P. 301.

119. R. S. Sharma, ***Indian Feudalism***: ***c. 300-1200***, Calcutta, 1965. PP. 1-60.

120. B.A.Saletore, *Op. Cit.,* P. 186.

121. ***SII,*** VII, No. 381.

122. *Ibid*, Nos. 223 and 325; B. Vasantha Shetty, "**Barkur- A Metropolitan City of Antiquity**" *Op. Cit.,* PP. 349-350.

123. K. V. Ramesh, ***A History of South Kanara***, *Op. Cit.,* PP. 276-277.

124. ***Ibid***, P. 289.

125. A.V. Narasimha Murthy, ***Vijayanagarada Nanya Sampattu***, Mysore, 1996, P. 20 and P. 25.

126. K. G. Vasanthamadhava, 'Some Observations on copper plate of Viranarasimha Sankaradevi in 1509 Saka' Unpublished paper presented in the Indian Archaeological X Annual Congress, Dharwar, 1978.

127. P. N. Narasimha Murthy, *Op. Cit.,*P. 481.

128. K. V. Ramesh, *Op. Cit.*, P. 277.

129. A. V. Narasimha Murthy, *Op. Cit.*, PP. 19, 20, 39, 51, 52.

130. K. G. Vasanthamadhava, 'Karavali Karnatakada Nanyagalu', *Op. Cit*, P. 80; ***SII***, VII, No. 336, 345.

131. *Ibid.*

132. ***SII***, VII, No. 201

133. ***ARSIE*** 1931-32, No. 266.

134. ***SII***, VII, No. 229.

135. A. V. Narasimha Murthy, *Op. Cit.*, P. 37.

136. *Ibid*, P. 480.

137. ***SII***, VII, No. 252.

138. ***SII***, VII, No. 364.

139. ***SII***, IX, Part II, No. 632.

140. K. G. Vasanthamadhava, ' Karavali Karnatakada Nanyagalu, *Op. Cit.,* P.81.

141. K. G. Vasanthamadhava, ***Trends in Karnataka Historical Research***, *Op. Cit,* PP. 35-37.

6

European Traders in South Kanara (1500-1763)

As in other parts of India, in South Kanara too there was the presence of European traders. This foreign element led to certain developments in the local economy. There was an increased demand for agrarian products like rice and spices like pepper. Due to increased trade the local merchants were able to realise more profit and accumulate capital and this they invested in the expansion of trade. The presence of Europeans certainly increased the production of commodities since the producers were obtaining more profit by the sale of goods to European traders. There began large scale production of commodities to be sent to places where there was substantial European presence. During this period the local traders were able to maintain their dominance and they competed with the foreign merchants. This was a period when there was the existence of pre-capitalist mode of production and the stage was set for the transition to capitalist mode of production. In the pre-colonial period the European powers were not militarily powerful. This was proved by the defeat of the Portuguese forces at the hands of the Nayakas of Keladi, who also challenged the power of the Dutch in Kerala. In fact the local kings used trade as a weapon and there were direct relations between trade and political relations. There was a great demand for the supply of rice, which was needed by the Europeans in Goa, Bombay and Malabar. There were instances of supply of provisions by the local kings to the Europeans after putting forward certain conditions. There was a great inflow of bullion into the region, which greatly improved the economic position of the traders. Due to the participation of the traders of the region in the world trade the economy reached the stage of capitalist mode of production. But this process of economic development was jeopardised due to the annexation of South Kanara to the Madras Presidency by the end of the eighteenth century. In this chapter an attempt is made to analyse the political relations between local kingdoms and the European powers in India, and their implications on trade, trade pattern, markets, mode of procurement of goods and other details related to trade.

The Portuguese, the Dutch and the English were the Europeans who came to South Kanara. However in the field of trade, the Portuguese presence was felt much more than the other Europeans upto 1799-1800. The Portuguese were the first to come to India. The activities of the Portuguese traders in India facilitated the transition of the economy from pre-capitalist mode of production to proto-capitalist mode of production. According to Amiya Kumar Bagchi, merchants exist in societies, which are not capitalist, and are not in the process of undergoing a transition to capitalism. They may even perform vital functions in a pre-capitalist society.[1] The Portuguese came to the orient in search of spices and to spread Christianity, but trade was given priority in their agenda. However, their religious leanings jeopardised their trade to some extent because the Portuguese had conflicts with the Muslims in the coasts of Malabar and South Kanara and this had certain debilitating impact on the coastal and overseas trade. Nevertheless it did not affect the fortunes of the traders of South Kanara. This was due to the increased dependence of the Portuguese on the Kanara coast for the supply of commodities since the 17th century. The supply line from the Malabar was cut off due to the antagonism between the Portuguese and the Muslims of Malabar. Thus the facts reveal that there were two phases in the Portuguese trade in South Kanara. While the first phase began in 1500 and ended in 1620, the second phase lasted from 1620 to 1763. During the initial phase the Portuguese trade with the traders of South Kanara was minimal and the Portuguese sources mention more about the Malabar trade than the Kanara trade. The Weberian approach argued that Portugal was in terms of institutions and mentalities far closer to Asia than to northern Europe. However, as stressed by

Sanjay Subrahmanyam our attempt should be to comprehend the changing scene within Asia and Europe. The political and commercial world of Asia into which the Portuguese entered in about 1500 was significantly different from that of 1700.[2] Further Sanjay Subrahmanyam stated that Asia before 1500 had broadly fallen into two categories; (1) agrarian based states and (2) trade based states. After 1500 the agrarian based states took more interest in maritime trade due to mercantilist spirit. After 1500 the quantitative dimensions of trade increased, so also the commodities traded, which came to include vast quantities of bullion and spices. It was in this changing context that the Portuguese operated.[3] The Portuguese *Estado da India* was basically a maritime state. Strategies of the Portuguese were directed towards maintenance of their control over the sea. Thus in the second half of 16th century only a few ports of the Kanara coast like Basrur, Mangalore and Honnavar were occupied by the Portuguese with their fortified settlements.[4] In fact the attempt of the Portuguese to find a sea route to India showed that they wished to maintain direct control over the maritime trade and the supply of spices.[5]

Dietmar Rothermund suggested that during the pre-industrial revolution period the European trade with the Asians led to favourable balance of trade for the Asian countries. This was due to the steady inflow of precious metals into Asia which, led to monetisation of the economy. But the capital that got accumulated was not invested in productive activities. It was due to the importance given to land revenue and the domination of the landed gentry. It was the Portuguese who first established their trade settlements in India. Most of the goods that they imported from India was labour intensive in nature - important among them being rice and pepper. Increased demand for these goods from the Europeans provided a fillip to their production. The Europeans were allowed to indulge in the private trade and the country trade and they entered the interiors to collect the goods and participate not only in the international trade but also in the internal trade.[6] The Europeans adjusted themselves to the already existing trade system in the coastal parts and tried to accumulate profit by competing with the local traders.

The debate regarding the role of the Portuguese in Asia was initiated by the Weberian scholar Jacob C. Van Leur who mentioned that the pattern of Portuguese commerce in Asia remained constant and there were only occasional changes in trade routes and volume of commodities.[7] Niels Steensgard supported the view of Van Leur when he stated that the Portuguese regime did not introduce a single new element into the commerce of South Asia.[8] Sanjay Subrahmanyam who studied the dynamics of the Portuguese-Asian trade and the growth of private traders criticised the above argument of the more or less static condition of trade for a long period of time.[9] He emphasised on the changing scene in both Asia and Europe. He analysed the transformation of agrarian based states into trade based states.[10] These details indicate that the scholars have discussed about the different dimensions of European trade in Asia. We intend to identify these connections and their implications in the context of South Kanara.

State and Trade

S. Arasaratnam observed that states and rulers in the seventeenth century were very receptive to European settlement for commerce in their dominions. They were influenced both by direct commercial consideration of the advantages each would bring, and also by diplomatic consideration of balancing one against the other. Indian states became adept at this latter game and learnt to effectively use European rivalry to maintain their freedom of commerce.[11] This diplomacy was in operation in the case of South Kanara. The local rulers utilised the rivalry between the Portuguese and the Arabs and between Europeans like the Dutch and the English. The state intervention brought capital into commerce, enlarged shipping capacity, provided protection when necessary, and promoted a climate favourable to commerce. It gave the merchants an access to political influence and they could persuade the rulers to act in the interest of commerce. However, the creation of monopolies and the policy of pre-emptive buying and forced sales disturbed the market and disturbed trade. These practices caused major price fluctuations in certain commodities. The attempt to control rice trade in Kanara by a few court favourites led to great increases in prices.[12] Further the fiscal policies of the state had the greatest impact on commerce. Duties were very low in most parts of India, from 3 per cent to 5 per cent, but appear to have been higher in Kanara where they could be 7 per cent or even 10 per cent.[13]

Treaties and Trade

On the eve of the arrival of the Portuguese, South Kanara was under the control of the Vijayanagara kings. The Vijayanagara rulers were interested in maritime trade in the fifteenth century itself. This fact is supported by the account of Abdul Razaq.[14] Due to the constant struggles between the Vijayanagara and the Bahamanis, there was always great demand for horses to be used in the wars. Hence, the Vijayanagara kings tried to maintain friendly alliances with the Portuguese. Because the Portuguese were active in the ports of western coast and they procured the horses from Arabia. They sold them to the Vijayanagara kings and gained huge profit.

In 1514 A.D. emperor Krishnadevaraya sent 'Ratelim Chetti', the Governor of Barkur to Goa and the latter is identified as Ratnappa Odeya. Ratnappa Odeya offered the Portuguese Viceroy 20,000 Sterlings for the exclusive right of buying 1,000 horses for Vijayanagara Empire. But the Viceroy Albuquerque declined the offer.[15] During the time of Krishnadevaraya an attempt was made by the Portuguese to get the help of Vijayanagara against their common enemy, namely the Bahamanis. But Krishnadevaraya did not agree to the proposal that he should allow the Portuguese to build fortress in Mangalore in return for the supply of horses.[16] The Portuguese attempted to encourage the Kanarese to trade with them and endeavoured to exclude other native traders from trading with them. Thus by a Charter of 21st October 1522 the king of Portugal freed the merchants of Bhatkal, Honnavar, Mangalore and Basrur from the entrance duty of 4.5 per cent which was

South Kanara in the 16th century showing the Travel route of Ludovico Varthema

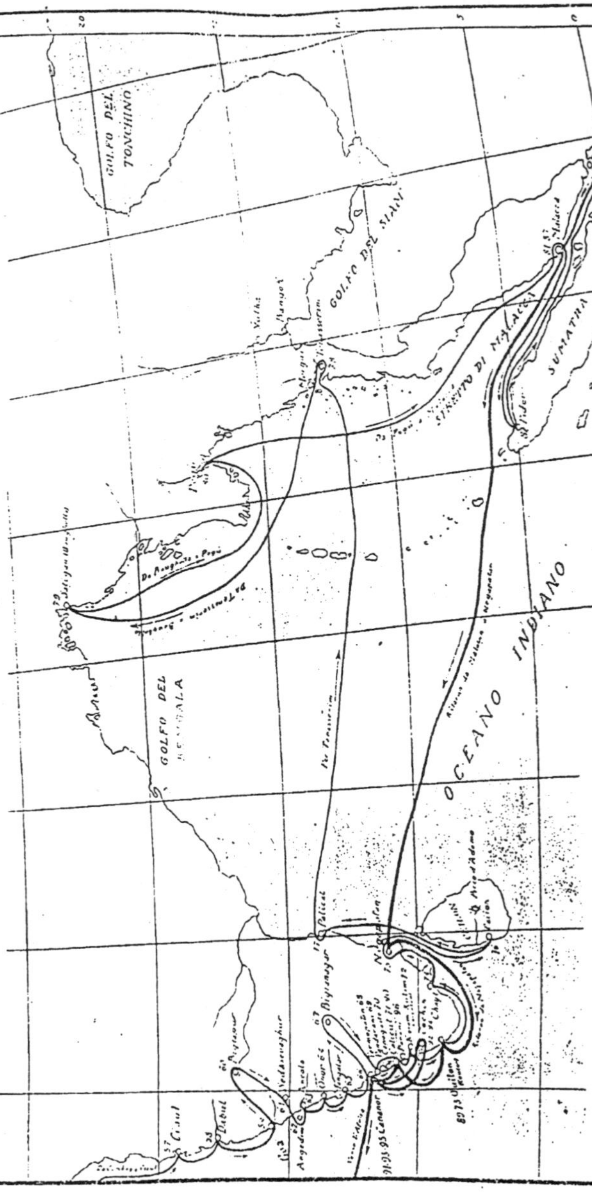

Source: Ludovico de Varthema, ***Itinerario***, Milan, 1956.

collected in respect of the articles entering Goa from other than Kanarese lands.[17] According to the treaty of 1546 signed between the Portuguese and the king of Vijayanagara, the latter was to compel all merchants in his kingdom trading with the coast to send their goods through Honnavar and Basrur. The factors and the merchants who were sent by the king of Portugal would buy these goods. Similarly the king of Vijayanagara should forbid the export of iron and saltpetre into the kingdom of Adilshah from any port or town of his own. And his merchants were compelled to bring their merchandise to the harbours of the kingdom of Vijyanagara where the Governors of India, not to cause them any harm would quickly purchase them.[18] The Portuguese were interested in gaining control over the supply of saltpetre, which was needed for the production of gunpowder. The treaty of 19th September 1547, signed between Joao de Castro, the Viceroy of Goa and the king of Vijayanagara, stipulated that the saltpetre extracted from various mines in the Vijayanagara kingdom was to be sold only to the Portuguese and was not to reach the territory of Sultan of Bijapur.[19] However it is said that the local chiefs did not quietly acquiesce to these arrangements. Default in payment of the grain tribute, followed by reprisals by fire and sword occurred from time to time.[20]

The Portuguese always tried to maintain control over the supply of certain vital items of trade like horses and saltpetre. Initially the Portuguese made use of their military superiority and destroyed some of the port complexes like Bhatkal, Basrur and Mangalore and other places on the western coast. They forced the local merchants to supply rice as tribute to the Portuguese. South Kanara consisted of several petty Chieftains who fought among themselves. The Portuguese interfered in the dispute between the Bangas and the Queen of Ullala and they took the side of the former. The conflict between the Portuguese and the Ullala Queen is well known. The support given to the Bangas helped the Portuguese in obtaining certain trade concessions like the non-payment of tolls for articles carried by boats in the rivers within his jurisdiction.[21] By the treaties with petty chieftains they were compelled to give a stipulated amount of rice and pepper loads as tribute (*pareas*) to the Portuguese. This exploitation by the Portuguese went unchecked during most of the sixteenth century.[22] The traders of Basrur had to pay annually five hundred loads of rice, the king of Barkur one thousand, the king of Karnad near Mulki eight hundred, the king of Mangalore 2,400 loads of rice and one thousand loads of oil, Manjeshwar seven hundred loads of rice and Kumbla eight hundred.[23] After the collapse of the Vijayanagara dynasty, the control of coastal parts of Karnataka had passed over to the Keladi or Ikkeri Nayakas, who pursued a more aggressive policy and after 1620 the Portuguese had to accept several peace treaties with the Nayakas of Ikkeri. The Keladi Nayakas realised the importance of the ports of South Kanara. In the year 1639 Virabhadra Nayaka shifted the seat of his government from Ikkeri to Bednur. Its situation was more favourable for trade as many important trade routes connecting the city of Mangalore and the Western ghats converged there.[24]

In the year 1620 the Portuguese signed a treaty with the Keladi ruler Venkatappa Nayaka (1592-1629). Accordingly, the Portuguese were to get the supply of rice and pepper from the Kanara coast. And the *casados* of Mangalore had to pay Venkatappa customs and other duties for the rice which they brought to the fortress from his territories, except for 500 bags of rice meant for their own consumption.[25] In March 1631 a treaty was signed between the Keladi king Virappa Nayaka and the Portuguese. This treaty consisted of the following clauses relating to trade:[26]

1. Virappa should cede to the Portuguese the peninsula of Gangolli, the Portuguese were allowed to possess and enjoy the place forever with its customary privileges.

2. Virappa and his successors should allow the Portuguese every year to cut and take away timber from the lands of Ikkeri. No duty should be imposed upon such timber.

3. The Ikkeri rulers should not admit into their port embarkation of the Malabarese nor should they allow the Malabarese to take sailors or food-grains from their ports and lands.

4. The taxes imposed on articles sold and purchased by the Portuguese should be discontinued. No duty should be imposed upon the ships from Muscat.

5. The lands and palm-groves belonging to the casados and other Portuguese residents near the fortress of Basrur should be ceded to Virappa. In return for these the latter should give, to the greater advantage of the former, land and income in Gangolli.

6. All the pepper should be sold without any obstruction to the purchaser or seller. The Viceroy should have no obligation to purchase pepper from Virappa; so also the latter should not be obliged to sell any to the former. However, if the Viceroy wished to purchase pepper and Virappa wished to sell it, it should be done according to the price fixed by free agreement between the two parties.

7. Virappa should be allowed to take from Goa every year ten horses, free of all duties, as long as the treaty of peace was maintained.

8. The Viceroy should hand over to Virappa two ships that were captured when there was hostility with Virabhadra Nayaka.

On 5th April another treaty was signed between the Keladi king Virabhadra Nayaka and the Portuguese which consisted of the following aspects:[27]

1. Virabhadra should release all the rice and other food-grains from the lands of Ikkeri and its ports to Goa.

2. He should command the merchants of upper Basrur to pay the customary annual tribute of 500 loads of rice to the Portuguese.

3. The Portuguese should compulsorily purchase from Virabhadra every year 350 *khandis* of pepper at the rate of 22 pagodas (Rs. 88/-) a *khandi*. In payment for this pepper he should accept the exchange rate of 102 *saotomes* for hundred *pagodas* of Ikkeri. If the Portuguese wished to purchase more

pepper it should be at a price fixed by agreement between them and Virabhadra.

4. Virabhadra should be allowed to take from Goa every year 12 horses of Arabia free of duties.

5. The Portuguese should give Virabhadra three passports every year for his embarkation to Mecca and Muscat, as was the custom before.

6. The Portuguese should be allowed to cut down and bring all the necessary wood from his territories without any payment for their shipyard. He should aid them in the process of cutting and transporting the wood.

7. He should instruct his tax collectors of the Kanara coast not to collect from the Portuguese more taxes than those imposed by his grandfather Venkatappa.

In 1671 a treaty was proposed and signed between the Keladi ruler Somashekhara Nayaka and the Portuguese with the following terms and conditions:[28]

1. The Portuguese would be given the sites for establishing factories and timber yards at Mangalore and Basrur.

2. The Portuguese should not establish oil mills at the sites.

3. They should use weights and measures of his kingdom.

4. He would order the merchants to pay the Portuguese factors the customary dues of anchorage and import and export duties. He would also order his custom officers to give the Portuguese the rice tributes.

5. The loading and unloading at the ports should be without unnecessary delay. The loading should be done in the presence of the custom officers. The relations between his officials and the Portuguese factors should be orderly and

peaceful. The Portuguese merchants, who sold goods at the ports, should pay him taxes.

6. The articles, which might be taken from his lands and which were meant for consumption at the factory would be exempt from taxation.

7. The boats, ships and *manchuas* of the Portuguese merchants, which came into his ports and sold their goods, would be given free passage to go back provided the sales tax was provided to him.

8. The ships carrying Portuguese passports should not be searched but should be given free navigation.

9. The embarkation of his lands should have free access into Portuguese ports, giving the embarkation good passage, but collecting due taxes from them.

10. His own ships carrying rice should not be subjected to pay any Portuguese taxes.

On 15 December 1678 another treaty was signed between the Keladi king Basavappa Nayaka and the Portuguese with the following terms:[29]

1. The Keladi king should give tributes as earlier in Mangalore and Basrur. The king should give the Portuguese a factory, together with surrounding grounds, at the port of Mangalore. He should supply at the site stone, lime, wood, free of cost to construct the factory. The Portuguese, however, would pay the officials employed in the construction of the factory.

2. The king should pay another tribute of 1500 bags of clean and good rice every year at the factory of Mangalore.

3. The factory or the timber yard of the Arabs should be razed to the ground. Henceforth the king should not allow the Arabs to trade at his ports and lands. If any Arab ship was found at his ports the Portuguese should be free to attack and capture it.

4. Ships belonging to the king or his vassals should not sail into the ports of the enemies of the Portuguese, particularly the Arab ports.

5. None of the king or his vassals should navigate without a Portuguese passport. A fee would be charged while issuing a passport, except for two passports for royal ships of the ruler. A passport issued by the factor of Mangalore was sufficient for ships navigating between Kanyakumari and Diu; but for ships sailing for Bengal or East Coast of India or the Red Sea strait or the Persian Gulf, passports should be obtained from the Secretary of State in Goa.

6. The factory of Mangalore should have all the privileges as if it was a fortress and former custom duty, anchorage and other customary taxes should be paid to the factor.

7. Within the factory compound the Portuguese should be allowed to have shops for tobacco, food grains and liquors. Five cargoes of provisions per day should be allowed to be taken to these shops free of tolls.

8. The Portuguese should be allowed to erect a church within their factory compound.

9. Fathers, missionaries and other Portuguese nationals who travelled through Kanara should be allowed free passage.

10. The Portuguese should be allowed to have warehouses for good grains within the factory compound. They should be allowed to have a fence and around the factory and possess guns.

11. The Portuguese merchants should be free to store their articles of trade within the factory compound. They should be required to pay taxes only on those articles, which they sold.

12. The factor should be allowed to bring free of imposts, whatever was necessary from the king's territories for consumption in the factory.

13. On the part of the Portuguese they should not establish oil mills.

14. Kanarese ships sailing into the ports of Goa should be subjected to nothing more than the customary dues.

15. The Portuguese Captains, Captain Majors of the fleets, convoying the ships of rice, should not compel the proprietors to give them loads of rice or any other bribe.

16. Basavappa, the king of Kanara should be given the license to fetch horses from Congo or Ormuz.

In February 1705 another treaty was signed between Basavappa Nayaka and the Portuguese with the following clauses:[30]

1. Basavappa should supply stone, lime, etc. for erecting a Portuguese factory in Mangalore.

2. He should pay an annual tribute of 1,500 bags of clean and white rice to the Portuguese.

3. Both Kanarese and Goan merchants should be permitted to take rice from Kanara for sale in Goa.

4. The import and export duties levied at the ports of Mulki and Manjeshwara should belong to the Portuguese.

Another treaty was signed between the Portuguese and Basavappa Nayaka in 1714 with the following clauses:[31]

1. The arrears of rice tributes amounting to 3,150 bags and the arrears of custom dues should be cleared.

2. The annual rice tribute should be raised from 1,500 to 1,900 bags.

3. The import and export duties should be paid to the Portuguese at Mangalore.

4. The Portuguese should be given preference, vis-à-vis other powers, in giving rice supplies; the Portuguese should never be denied such supplies; Kanarese and Portuguese

merchants and their ships carrying rice should be allowed free passage between Goa and Kanara.

5. Each of the rice bags taken by the merchants of Mangalore to Goa should measure 2 *maos* and 7 *curos* , each *curo* being eight measures.

6. He should order Upendra Kamath, former custom officer of Mangalore, to pay the dues of import and export duties to the factor of Mangalore.

7. The Factor of Mangalore should be free to purchase wood and send it to Goa.

8. Kaddase Dammarasa Prabhu, ambassador of Basavappa, should maintain a *Saraf* at Goa to weigh and test the gold to be taken to Kanara.

9. Basavappa's subjects were not to pay tolls at the fortresses and the lands of the Portuguese.

10. No oil mill should be established in the factory.

11. Kanarese ships, which were sent to Goa with cargo of rice, should not be maltreated there.

The Keladi king Shivappa Nayaka fought fierce wars against the Portuguese and achieved victory. The Portuguese, when they were militarily superior, tried to dictate the terms of treaty upon native rulers. But when the Keladi kings defeated the Portuguese, the latter had to accept exorbitant prices of rice and pepper. The Portuguese maintained their trade contacts with ports of South Kanara mainly to obtain continuous supply of rice and pepper. They also traded in ginger, iron and saltpetre. The above treaties indicate that the Saraswat Brahmin community had emerged as prominent trading community on the Kanara coast. The Portuguese tried to protect their interest by initially using military force and later they did this by signing treaties with native rulers. Thus some of the major treaties concluded between the Portuguese and the Keladi rulers indicate the changes that were taking place in trade between the two political powers. The Keladi kings tried to protect the

Ports of the Western coast during the 16th century

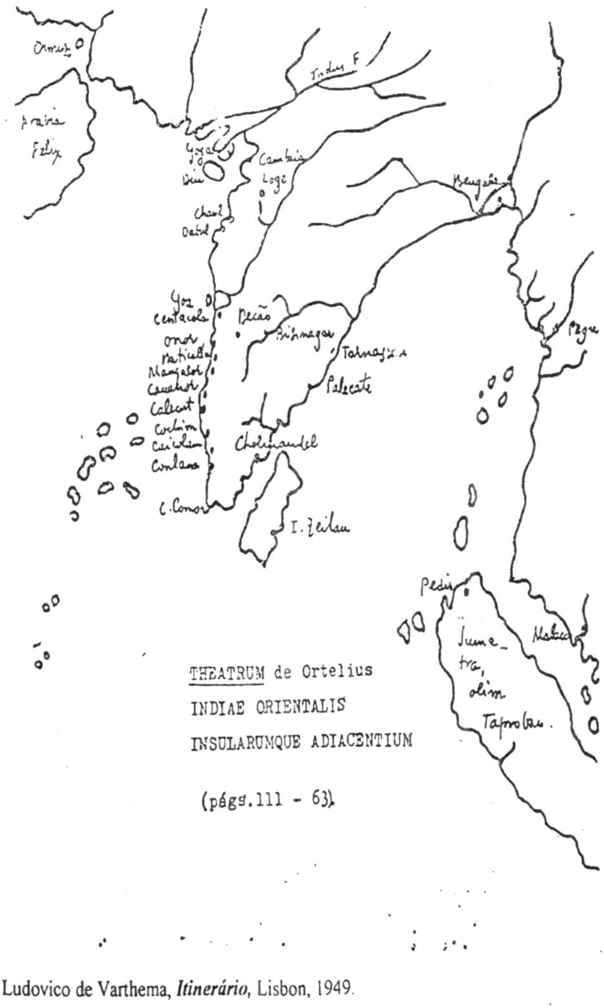

Source: Ludovico de Varthema, *Itinerário*, Lisbon, 1949.

economic interests of their state by creating a more favourable condition for trade. These interests of the rulers made them control urban centres and ports of South Kanara. The Keladi rulers not only protected the native traders, most of whom belonged to the Saraswat Brahmin community, but also tried to promote the maritime trade. The king, as any other merchant, bargained with the Portuguese to sell his goods at a higher price. The sale of essential commodities like rice was considered as a political weapon to subjugate the Portuguese since the latter mostly depended on the rice supplies from the Kanara ports, particularly Mangalore and Basrur.

Rice Trade

South Kanara was basically an agrarian region and was known for paddy cultivation. Rice was the staple food consumed by the people of this region from very early times. But there was always surplus production and export of rice. Portuguese depended heavily on the supply of rice from the ports of Mangalore and Basrur. These ports exported rice to other ports in India and also to overseas ports. The Portuguese tried to maintain constant rice supplies from Kanara by signing treaties with the kings. But the local rulers for want of higher price often violated these treaties. In 1518 A.D. Duarte Barbosa recorded that Barkur possessed good quantity of rice which was exported in ships to Malabar and foreign countries. He observed that the merchants carried rice to Ormuz, Aden, Xaer, Cannanore and Calicut, and they bartered it for copper, coconuts and molasses. In Malabar there was great demand for rice since rice was the staple food of the people of this region also.[32] Barbosa stated that from the port of Mangalore many ships took cargoes of black rice, which was better and more wholesome than the white, and sold in the land of Malabar. Cargoes of this rice were taken in many ships of the Muslims to Aden.[33] From Kumbla bad quality black rice was taken by the traders of Malabar who sold it to low class people, who needed rice at a cheaper rate. They also took such a cheaper quality rice to the Maldive islands and sold them to the inhabitants there who were generally poor and therefore preferred the black rice than the white one. [34] There existed trade between the kingdom of Eli in Malabar and Kanara ports like Barkur and Basrur. The rice cargoes that were sent from Barkur and Basrur were stored in Cannanore and Dharmapatam.[35]

Throughout the sixteenth and seventeenth centuries Goa demonstrated how heavily dependent it was on Kanara for rice. About 3 to 4 convoys left Kanara for Goa every year in the sixteenth century.[36] Basrur exported an annual average of 19,75,000 kilograms of rice during 1611-16, 15,30,000 kilograms in 1623 and an average of 2,75,00,000 kilograms per annum during September 1625 to March 1628.[37] In the seventeenth century there was an increase in the demand for rice. This was due mainly to the prevailing circumstances rather than to profitability. It was never an item of export to Portugal. Normally, the Portuguese bought rice for the provisioning of fortresses and factories on the western coast of India. They also procured it for the Persian Gulf ports of Muscat, the Swahili states, Ceylon, Malacca, etc. The Portuguese traded in three qualities of rice, namely, high quality, medium quality and low quality. High quality of rice was produced in bulk in the regions of Basrur and Mangalore.[38] The principal export from Basrur and Mangalore was rice, used for provisioning the viceregal capital, its ports and its fleets. According to Bocarro, Basrur and Mangalore together comprised 'the sole granary from which Goa, Malacca, Muscat, Mozambique and Mombasa are supplied'. A. R. Disney opined that while this claim was exaggerated, rice from these outlets was undoubtedly vital to the Portuguese especially during drought years such as the early 1630's.[39] The supply of rice was used as a weapon by the Keladi Nayakas to force the Portuguese to purchase pepper. The Keladi king Virabhadra Nayaka demanded a high price for pepper. In order to pressurise the Portuguese he blockaded rice supplies to them from his territories. The Viceroy-in-Council on 17th January 1636 decided to purchase food grains from the ports of Manjeshwara and Kumbla. Though these ports belonged to Virabhadra, the people there sold their rice to anyone who paid for it.[40] When there was conflict between the Portuguese and the Keladi ruler Shivappa Nayaka, there was scarcity of food grains in Goa. The Municipality of Goa submitted a memorandum urging the Governor to conclude peace with the greatest speed that was possible. The memorandum pointed out that the food supplies of the Keladi territories were important for the sustenance of Goa and for the Portuguese soldiers waging war against the Dutch at Ceylon and other places.[41] During 1628-29 the Portuguese obtained rice supplies with the help of Kanarese merchant Vitula Nayak who sent rice from Basrur. In 1628 his agents brought rice worth 21,462 *ashrafis* to the Goa port from Kanara. In Mangalore Rama Kini had good reputation among the rice contractors.[42]

The price of rice in the 1620's and 1630's[43] is presented in the following table and the fluctuation therein is shown in the next diagram.

Table-1

Price of High Quality Rice in Kanara:

Year	**Price per quintal** (in *xerafins*)
1628	1.50
1631	1.75
1635	2.40
1639	1.98

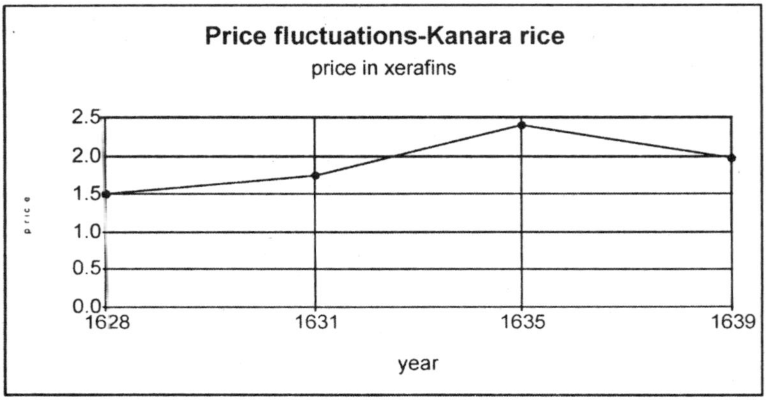

The above table and diagram show that there were fluctuations in the price of rice perhaps depending on the political and economic conditions of the period. The rice trade led to inflow of bullion into South Kanara. Ships of merchants were frequently employed to fetch rice or to send the cash for rice. For example, in the year 1630, 4000 *saotomes* in gold were sent to Basrur in a *naveta mourisca* (a ship belonging to a Muslim merchant), accompanied by another ship owned by Antonio Carreira Salema. In return they were to bring rice from there.[44] The attempt made by the Portuguese to establish their fortress in Gangolli was to enable them to get continuous supply of rice at a reasonable price.

Sanjay Subrahmanyam made a study of the rice trade in Basrur. According to him only the traders of Basrur regularly supplied rice tributes to the Portuguese. From the 1560s onwards Kanara became the lifeline of Goa, a region that was dependent on outside sources for its supply of foodstuff, particularly rice. Regular convoys of rice-bearing ships began to traverse the coast from the Kanara ports to Goa often escorted by ships from the Goa fleet.[45] The chief group on whom the tax's incidence occurred was the native merchants, or 'chatins' of Basrur. This rice was carried in small open vessels down the river from the native town. These boats had to pass the Portuguese fort located at the mouth of the estuary and were required to make payment of the levy at that point. These boats normally sailed in large fleets, and in 1630's there were as many as 150 such boats in a single fleet from Kanara to Goa.[46] An estimate for the 1630's provided by Antonio Bocarro states that the value of rice carried from all parts of Kanara to Goa in the main annual convoy was worth some 3,00,000 *xerafins*. The Basrur-Goa flow was only a fraction of the total Kanara-Goa flow.[47]

The Portuguese were very anxious to maintain a continuous flow of rice to their fort at Muscat. In 1629, a large order of over 5,00,000 kilograms was placed by the administration with Vithula Nayak, a Saraswat merchant who had participated actively in the economy of Portuguese India. Again some 1,15,000 kilograms were dispatched from Basrur in early 1631 to Muscat in the pinnace of one Antonio de Serra Marchao in response to urgent demands from the garrison there.[48] In 1634 a consignment of unstated dimensions was procured and dispatched to the Portuguese ports in Mozambique from Basrur.[49] In early 1635, for the provisioning of the state's armadas, which were outward bound from Goa to various destinations in Asian waters, a large order was placed for rice with the Kanarese merchant Rama Kini, who procured rice from Mangalore and Basrur.[50] In the following decade and up to 1650, occasional consignments of rice were also sent from Basrur on the Estado's initiative to Ceylon and Malacca.[51] The two types of rice that were exported from South Kanara were *jirigai*, the high quality rice, which was sent as tribute to the Portuguese, and the *amutti*, a coarse, black-grained type. In 1650's high quality rice was available in Kanara at 8 *xerafins* a *khandi*. The same rice was sold in Muscat at 15 *xerafins*. Sanjay Subrahmanyam analyses that the profits on a single voyage would not have been very large if rice alone was carried. A frequently observed pattern was to use the rice as ballast, while carrying other more profitable goods as well.[52] Nevertheless, we should remember that rice was the main commodity produced in Kanara. In this context we suggest that since the Portuguese could be forced to pay more price for rice, perhaps a single voyage of rice alone was also profitable.

The following diagrams throw light on the export of rice from Kanara to Ceylon[53], Basrur to Muscat[54], and Kanara to Goa[55].

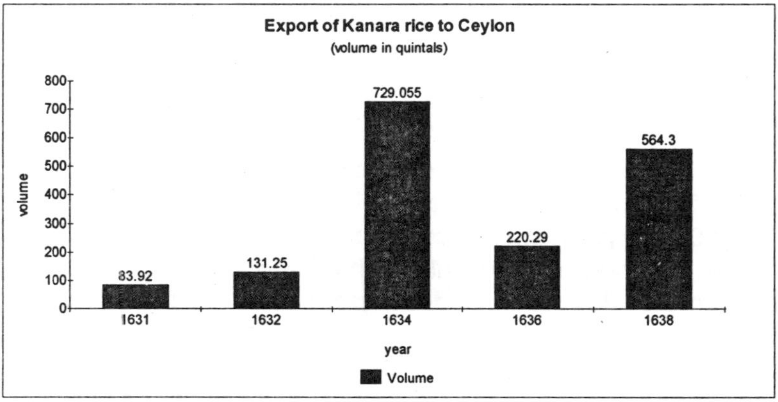

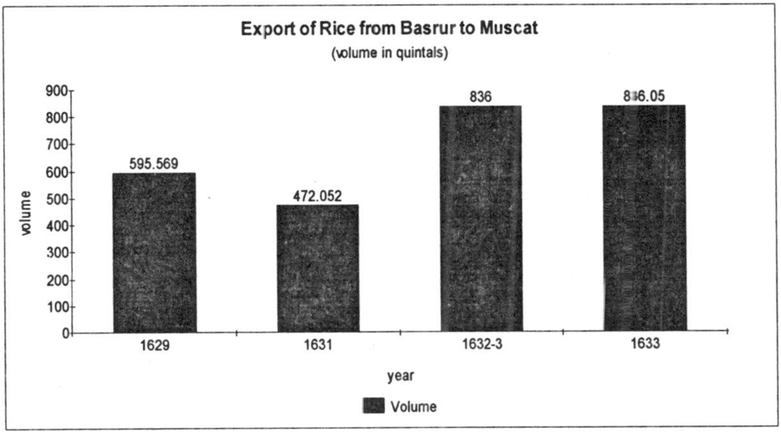

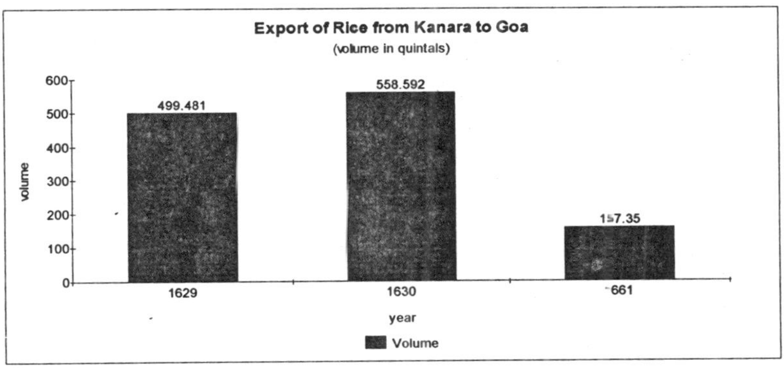

Pepper Trade

The ports of South Kanara were well connected by roads with the hinterland centres where there was the production of pepper. The traders procured pepper by contacting the producers in different parts of South Kanara and the Western ghat region. Pepper was one of the important items of export from South Kanara, particularly Mangalore and Basrur. The pepper produced in South Kanara was costlier than that of the

Malabar pepper but due to political exigencies the Portuguese after 17th century had to depend on the Kanara ports for the procurement of pepper. The Portuguese did not like those who maintained contact with the Arabs. But the traders of South Kanara entertained those traders who provided them higher profit. It is for this reason that they were ready to face the wrath of the Portuguese.

The Portuguese practice was to arrange contracts with individual merchants and syndicates. In 1602 Antonio Mendes de Tomar and Antonio Fernandes de Sampaio were contracted to supply the Portuguese in Kanara with pepper, and in 1603 an Indian goldsmith and his nephew agreed to supply 1,500 quintals of pepper at Honnavar and Basrur. During the time of Keladi Venkatappa Nayaka the Portuguese purchased most of the pepper they needed from Kanara. The various contractors acquired their stocks of pepper either by sending their own agents to buy in the producing areas, or indirectly from the lesser middlemen. Usually pepper was bought during the period from March to May.[56] The weighing, assessing and handing over of pepper took place at a closed market attended by Portuguese trade officials, officials representing the local rulers, and traders selling pepper. Each of the principal exporting towns had a weighing house set aside for these transactions. These buildings were at points of easy access to river transport. There were officials to inspect the quality of pepper since the traders sometimes mixed immature pepper with mature pepper to get more profit. But it led to the loss of weight when the pepper consignments reached Portugal. By the beginning of the second half of the sixteenth century the Portuguese experienced increasing rates of loss of weight on their pepper. A major cause was their attempt to control the price of pepper during inflation which forced the suppliers in India to offer low quality or adulterated stock in an effort to cut their own costs.[57] In the early seventeenth century the loss of weight incurred by pepper in transit between Malabar and Kanara factories and Goa averaged only about 3 per cent.[58]

According to A.R.Disney although the Portuguese pepper

supplies from Malabar and Kanara were bought through middlemen, the procedure itself was not exclusively commercial. In these areas the Portuguese tried to organise their pepper trade on the basis of political agreements with the petty Indian states. They preferred the local rulers to take responsibility for the safe passage of the pepper. In order to maintain good relations with the officials and the rulers, the Portuguese gave them gifts. In the ports of Basrur and Mangalore it was not the Portuguese who paid the custom duties, but rather the traders who supplied pepper. However, the Portuguese gained no real price advantage from this arrangement and invariably paid more for the good quality Kanara pepper than for Malabar pepper. From 1610's onwards the Portuguese were obliged to purchase most of their pepper from the Nayakas of Ikkeri.[59] Pepper was normally paid for by the Portuguese either in local silver coinages as specified in the treaties with the rulers of the pepper port or in gold. For the purchase of Kanara pepper the Portuguese usually had to obtain Vijayanagara *pagodas* which were required for transactions with the Nayakas of Ikkeri. Sometimes uncoined gold was transferred directly from Goa to the pepper ports.[60] From the second decade of the seventeenth century, the Portuguese bought most of their pepper supplies in Kanara. Between 1612 and 1629 twice as much pepper was exported from Kanara to Lisbon as from Malabar. Pepper prices in Kanara were consistently higher than in Malabar and despite some fluctuations from year to year, showed an increase that amounted to between 30 and 40 per cent.[61] However the Kanara pepper was of higher quality than the Malabar pepper. During the second decade of the seventeenth century pepper export fluctuated between 5,000 quintals to 11,500 quintals per year. The average export during this period was around 9,100 quintals per year. It is said that this meant an increase of 15 per cent when compared with the earlier decade. The total export of pepper consisted of 70.5 per cent of Kanara pepper as against 29.5 per cent from Malabar and Malacca.[62] There were major fluctuations in prices during the period from 1611 to 1650. The price of pepper in Kanara in 1611 was 15.5 *ashrafis* per quintal and by 1622 it rose to 19.5 *ashrafis*. Afzal Ahmad wrote that the reason for this fluctuation in prices was the rivalry between

European companies and the forced sale policy of the Keladi rulers.[63] He provided details on the fluctuation in the price of pepper as given below.[64]

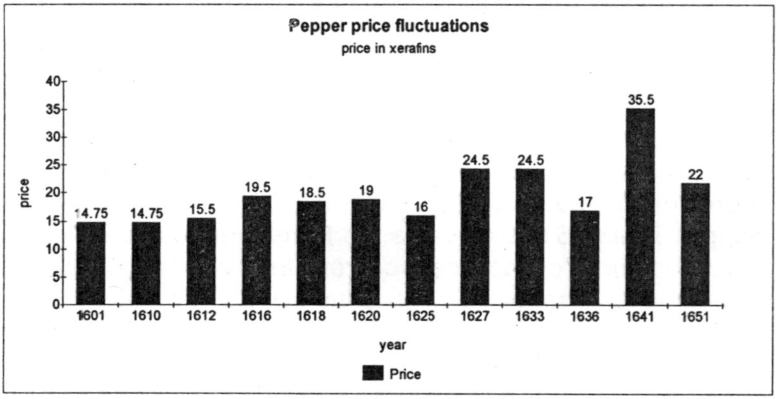

Another reason for the increased price of pepper in Kanara was that there were free markets in this region where Asian merchants made their major purchases for various Asian markets. The Surat and Dabhul merchants were the major buyers there, away from Portuguese control and taxation, for Gujarat, Hindustan and West Asian markets. Also Arab and Persian merchants sailed to Kanara and traded in pepper. All these factors explain the increased price of pepper in Kanara. The hinterland political powers, well aware of the advantages they had, strove to keep the trade free from outside interference and kept a tight control on the commercial process. The availability of rice was also a great attraction to Gujarati, Arab and Persian traders, who were thus able to procure here the staples for the India-West Asia trade.[65] By the beginning of seventeenth century, much of the pepper from Malabar and Kanara was exported to Surat where Malabar and Kanarese traders were assured of getting the best price. With or without Portuguese *cartazes*, a growing volume of shipping plied between Surat and Kanarese ports of Honnavar, Bhatkal and Basrur.[66]

The acquisition of Kanara ports proved crucial to the Portuguese for the procurement of pepper. It was not until 1580s and 1590s that the Kanara pepper began to account for a significant proportion of pepper cargoes on Lisbon bound India men. After 1600 the importance of Kanara ports in the Portuguese network was enhanced. With the loss of Pepper supply from Malabar and the increasing aggression by the Dutch it was necessary for the Portuguese to maintain the link between Kanara and Goa.[67] Thus the ports of South Kanara gained considerable significance during the seventeenth century.

Merchants and Their Methods

The rice trade in Kanara was carried on by three groups of traders. These were the official traders of the Portuguese *Estado da India*, private Portuguese and *mestico* traders and the Kanarese and other merchants.[68] In the first half of the seventeenth century the Portuguese Government in Goa took a direct part in the proceedings primarily to ensure the supply of foodstuff to Portuguese possessions. This meant the dispatch of money from Goa to the Portuguese captains of the various forts. The captain would then procure the rice from either a local merchant or a Portuguese private trader, and dispatch the rice to its destination.[69] Each fortress had a factory with a Factor. At the time of loading and unloading of ships, the factory employed more personnel for this work. All the officials of a factory were under the authority of a Factor. Before the loading of ships, he was to prepare a log of the commodities to be sent to the capital and obtain a receipt of the same from the Captain or the Factor of the ships.[70] Normally the pepper bought for export to Portugal was acquired from middlemen at weighing houses and factories in Kanara and later sent to Goa. The middlemen who brought the dried pepper from the cultivators transported it by the cart, oxen or river boat to the markets inland or on the coast, and sold it there to distributors and exporters. Most middlemen were independent operators, but some acted as agents for wealthy coastal merchants.[71] The economic subordination of the pepper cultivators is suggested by the fact that they were frequently forced to pledge their pepper in advance to the middlemen. In the early sixteenth century the middlemen in each season acquired the next season's crop either for cash advance or in exchange for cotton clothes, and other goods, which they stored at the seaports. Usually the Portuguese authorities bought the pepper from middlemen or contractors after a small or half payment of the total amount. The remaining amount was to be paid after the arrival of ships with money from Portugal.[72]

Other Items of Trade

Basrur was an exporter of coir, small amount of pepper, fair quantities of saltpetre, gunpowder, iron, imported from over the Ghats via the Haidergarh pass, and even a small amount of fine textiles, whose use was particularly preferred in the Persian Gulf region. The Portuguese also collected saltpetre from Kanara. Vitula Nayaka was a prominent merchant who procured saltpetre and sold it to the Portuguese.[73] There was trade in coconut. The copper plate inscription dated Saka 1603 from Kodladi (Kundapur Taluk) mentions about coconut plantation on the Gangolli sea- shore. The Keladi kingdom had trade relations with the Portuguese, Dutch and English Companies. Great demand for coconut from them resulted in an increased coconut cultivation. Even the lands like '*bele*' not useful for raising any other crop were brought under coconut cultivation. This inscription reveals that the state used to take initiative in planting coconuts because it brought more income to the state treasury. The state advocated the enhancement of maritime trade.[74] Tobacco was cultivated in Basrur and there might have existed trade in tobacco.[75] Other articles of trade which the Portuguese secured from the region were sugar, iron, ginger, coir, saltpetre, wood and timber.[76] In 1683, the Factor of Mangalore was instructed to purchase coir from Maldives for the stock of the Mangalore warehouse, which was later to be sent to Goa.[77] In exchange for the articles of trade which they purchased in Kanara, the Portuguese sold there several articles which they brought with them from Portugal and other countries. Horses, copper, quick silver, vermilion, coral, lead and salt were the important articles which they sold in Kanara.[78] The Portuguese factory was a centre of trade, a military post and a centre of missionary activities. The Portuguese ships were loaded with rice, saltpetre, sandalwood, timber, pepper and other articles of trade at the port of Mangalore. Such ships sailing from Goa to China, Macao and Bengal anchored at Mangalore for supplies of merchandise, marines, and convoys. The Portuguese supplied ammunitions, salt, mirrors, etc. to the people of Kanara.[79] Alexander Hamilton stated that the Portuguese had 6 or 8 ships stationed in Basrur. These ships carried their cargoes of rice to Muscat and brought back horses, dates, pearl and other merchandise produced in Arabia.[80]

Urbanisation of Ports

The policy of the Keladi state to give importance to maritime trade led to the urbanisation of coastal port towns like Basrur and Mangalore. The initial policies of the Portuguese did not promote the growth of trade centres as urban centres. In order to establish hegemony over the coastal ports, the Portuguese made use of violence. In 1530 the Portuguese under the command of Nuno da Cunha crossed the river of Mangalore which flowed through the Ullal territory and destroyed the stockade and fortified possessions. This was done with the purpose of punishing a rich merchant of that place, who was in league with the King of Calicut against them.[81] In the year 1556, Dom Alvaro de Silveyra was sent at the head of several vessels against the Queen of Ullal for refusing to pay the ordinary tribute. The city of Mangalore was plundered and a gorgeous Hindu temple was destroyed. In another such attack the Portuguese assaulted the city, set it on fire and cut down its grove of palm trees.[82] In 1558 the Portuguese exhibited their brutality to the people of Mangalore. In that year the Portuguese Commander Luiz de Mello da Silva learnt that a ship belonging to the Muslims of Cannanore was anchored at

Mangalore. De Mello entered the city and put to sword all those whom he confronted, without discriminating between men and women, old and young. They thought that these atrocities were necessary to terrorise the enemies.[83] The merchants opposed the Portuguese atrocities. In Basrur the traders responded by boycotting the supply of rice to Goa and in a petition sent to the Portuguese Viceroy it was stated that due to Portuguese atrocities some traders started migrating from Basrur to other safer places.[84] The wars that were fought between the Portuguese and the native people led to the destruction of some urban settlements. Also the Arabs and Marathas under Shivaji, Kanhoji Angria and later Tulaji Angria attacked the ports of Kanara. Shivaji attacked Basrur in the year 1665 and carried away 800,000 guilders.[85] In 1695 the Arabs came with a fleet and plundered the seacoast of Kanara, and burnt Barkur and Mangalore and carried away a great booty.[86]

But in the seventeenth century trade between Kanarese ports and Goa facilitated urbanisation of the coastal ports. When the Ikkeri kingdom established its hegemony on the coast, it began to support merchant settlement in its ports. The Ikkeri ports of Basrur and Mangalore attracted large number of merchants. These merchants were Kannada and Komatti Chettis, and Saraswat Brahmans. Mapilla Muslims came there from Malabar to trade more freely, away from Portuguese pressure. Konkani merchants were mainly involved in coastal trade northwards and southwards upto Surat and Srilanka respectively. They traded in pepper, rice and coconut products. Saraswat Brahmans found a favourable haven in Goa, where the Portuguese enticed them with privileges to ensure the port's rice supply. These merchants traded under Portuguese protection along the coast from Diu to Cochin. Their coastal shipping was a major constituent of the *kafilas* escorted by the Portuguese in and out of Goa. There was entry of previously non-commercial communities into commerce to take advantage of the new opportunities. The court officials of the Ikkeri kingdom virtually monopolised rice trade.[87] The following chart gives details of number of Portuguese ships stationed on the Kanara coast:[88]

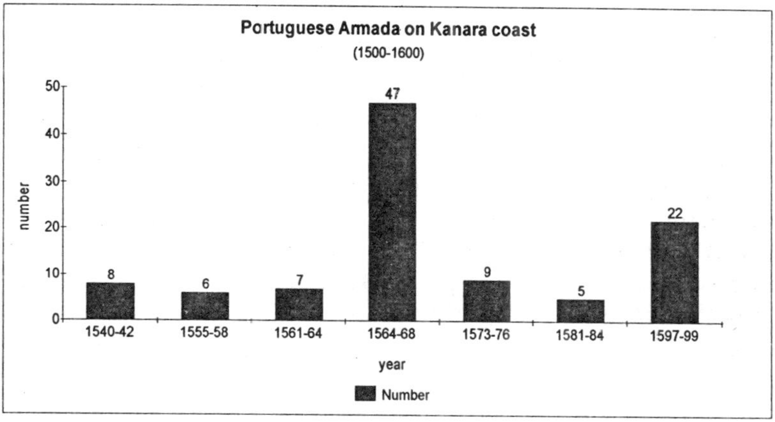

The construction of forts led to urbanisation of the ports of South Kanara. Administrative arrangements were made in these forts. Each fort consisted of officials like Captain, Factor, Writer, Judges, Surgeon, Interpreter, Chief of artillery, Door keeper, Chief of peons and Church officials. This administrative system involved significant amount of financial expenditure for the Portuguese.[89] In these ports there was the settlement of the *casados*. In 1635, in Basrur there lived 35 *casados* outside the fortress. Each *casado* had a slave who accompanied him, carrying the master's arms. The habitation of the *casados*[90] was surrounded by a mud-wall, 3.3 metres high with watch-towers in the form of bulwarks. The *casados* possessed some rice fields and palm trees outside the habitation. When there was peace they enjoyed the products of their possessions.[91] It is stated that a settlement of about thirtyfive families of the *casados* existed in Mangalore as per the Portuguese record of the year 1656. The settlement was situated very close to the fort. The houses were built of stone and lime having tiled rocks. The *casados* in Gangolli had a church near the fort.[92] According to Alexander Hamilton in Mangalore there existed a pretty church and there resided great number of black Christians. He criticised the clergy as the "very scum of Christianity" because they thought that whoring, thieving and murder were no sins if they could be benefited from them.[93]

It is said that the merchants themselves administered the port of Basrur. The chronicler Couto stated that unlike other regions along the coast, the settlers of Basrur governed themselves like a republic and paid some tributes to the Raya (king). The power in the city is described as being in the hands of a collective of 'governadores' or 'regedores', who on specific occasions appointed agents from the merchant community to prosecute negotiations.[94]

The construction of churches enhanced the urban character of the port towns. Portuguese fortress or factory was accompanied by the construction of a chapel or a church. The Portuguese authorities used priests and missionaries in diplomatic negotiations, including commercial dealings.[95] In the 1520s, the Franciscans managed to establish a mission in Mangalore. As a result they established three churches in the region: Nossa Senhora do Rosario (Our Lady of the Rosary) in Mangalore, Nossa Senhora das Merces (Our Lady of Mercy) in Ullal, and Sao Francisco de Assis in Farangipet.[96] The above details show that the Portuguese though initially were responsible for the destruction of certain urban settlements, subsequently contributed to urbanisation of some of the ports by the construction of forts, houses and churches with their distinct architectural style.

Cartazes

The *cartazes* or passport system indicated the attempt of the Portuguese to regulate the trade on the Western coast. They tried to prevent the competitors like the Arabs from trading with the Kanara ports and taking away rice and spices, which were needed for the Portuguese settlements. However, the Portuguese were never able to completely implement the *cartazes* system because of the hostile attitude of the Mapilla traders of Malabar and their contacts with Arabs.

A *cartaz* was valid only for one year. A fee had to be paid to the Portuguese for obtaining it.[97] The fee was higher if the ship was to undertake an overseas trade and it was lower for the one engaged in coastal trade. *Cartazes* were issued only in Goa for overseas trade. They could be obtained at any Portuguese factory or fortress for coastal trade.[98] The contents of Portuguese *cartaz* could be divided into two categories. Firstly, it specified the name of the vessel, its owner, the number of masts, its tonnage, equipment, crew, pilot, captain, guns mounted, number of soldiers, etc. Secondly, it laid down a number of conditions which the grantee of a *cartaz* had to observe. If any of the conditions was violated the ship concerned was liable to confiscation with all the goods and crew on board. These conditions were:[99]

1. The ship should not trade in or carry on board such articles, which were royal monopolies like pepper, horses, etc.

2. It should not carry on board any Christian slave.

3. It should not sail into the ports of the enemies of the Portuguese.

4. It should sail into a certain port first and then to other permissible ones.

In 1602 the Portuguese issued a *cartaz* to one trader from Basrur to take rice to Hormuz. In 1621 another *cartaz* was issued to a trader of Basrur to take a ship with 800 *khandis*. According to Sanjay Subrahmanyam, this *cartaz* demonstrated some of the classic features of the period: a ship owned by a Hindu merchant, but whose *nakhauda* was a Muslim, on which space was freighted by a large number of small merchants.[100] However, after 1700 majority of the *cartazes* issued by the Portuguese, as mentioned in the two volumes of *Livro do Cartazes*, were given to the Kanarese merchants.

Details of Cartazes issued to Kanarese Merchants:[101]

Year	Merchant	Volume	Destination
1705	Ramanna Ballagi Kallianpur.	300	Kanara to Surat
1705	Ranbaca Guzarate Surat	300	Mangalore to Mecca
1707	Vittula Cumballa Codiyalla	50	Mangalore to Aden
1707	King of Kanara	300	Basrur to Congo & Bassora.
1707	Paddiar	150	Basrur to Mecca
1707	Custa Paddiar Basrur	125	Basrur to Serdefar
1707	Sidy Basavayya Bidrur	125	Basrur to Serdefar
1708	Sidy Basavayya Bidrur	200	Basrur to Congo
1708	Sedua Naique	400	Basrur to Surat
1708	Vanttadas Satanagi Bidanur	800	Mangalore to Surat, Barra Araba, and Bengal
1708	Vassadas Qatanagy Bidanur	250	Mangalore to Baracabe
1708	Chica Ahmad Bary Mangalore	350	Mangalore to Congo
1709	Babu Hedago Basrur	150	Basrur to Surat, Mecca & Congo
1709	Custa Paddiar	125	Basrur to Surat,

	Basrur		Mecca and Congo
1709	Custa Paddiar Basrur	150	Basrur to Congo
1709	Nimanaya Chatim Basrur	275	Basrur to Congo
1709	Sidy Basavaya Basrur	150	Basrur to Congo, Serdefar
1709	Vistudas Guzarate Kanara	350	Mangalore to Honnavar, Surat and Mecca
1709	Vengatty Comaty Panduranga Sinay Goa	350	Goa to Manglore, Mecca and Aden
1709	Vistudas Guzarate	800	Manglore to Honnavar, Mecca
1709	Xeque Aly Binsultan de Abdul Xeque	600	Manglore to Surat, Congo
1709	Mulam Abdul Gafar Surat	1500	Manglore to Surat, Malacca
1710	Rama Poy Kanara	300	Manglore to Ormuz
1710	Basavaya Bedrur	155	Basrur to Ormuz
1710	Vistudas Guzarate Kanara	1200	Honnavar to Calicut, Surat, Bengal
1710	Adbul Rahiman Basrur	150	Basrur to Ormuz, Congo
1710	Santa Virapa Bedrur	125	Basrur to Xerdefar, Ormuz

1710	Custa Paddiar	125	Basrur to Bassora
1710	Bapu Hegaddo Basrur	150	Basrur to Mecca
1710	Gurapa Bedrur	125	Basrur to Ormuz
1710	Nimanaya Bedrur	275	Basrur to Ormuz
1710	Sirlu Naique Basrur	100	Basrur to Ormuz
1710	Sidy Basavaya Bedrur	275	Basrur to Xerdafar, Ormuz
1710	Ranganna Bagatu Basrur	100	Basrur to Ormuz
1711	Amada Caca Mangalore	200	Manglore to Mecca
1711	Bapu Heggaddo Basrur	200	Basrur to Mecca
1711	Vittu Paddiar	150	Basrur to Ormuz
1711	Rama Poy Cundapur	200	Basrur to Aden
1711	Sidy Basavaya	250	Basrur to Xerdufar
1711	Bastur Sir Naique Basrur	100	Basrur to Aden
1711	Ramachandra Pandito Minister of King of Sunda	300	Basrur to Mecca
1711	Guru Raya Bidanur	125	Basrur to Mecca
1711	Ranaganna Bagata Basrur	100	Basrur to Sinde
1711	King of Kanar	800	Ports of Kanara to Congo, Bassora

1712	Musse Mangalore	300	Mangalore to Congo
1712	Sidy Basavaya Bidanur	175	Basrur to Congo
1712	Sidy Basavaya Bidanur	250	Basrur to mecca
1712	Ranganna Bagata Basrur	100	Basrur to Xerdufar
1712	Damarasa Naique Basrur	125	Basrur to Xerdufar
1713	Saida Ally Ancola	150	Basrur to Aden
1713	Hafil Hamad Salim Surat	600	Mangalore to Ormuz
1713-14	Saida Miram Ancola	150	Basrur to Aden
1713-14	Saida Ally Ancola	150	Karwar to Basrur, Aden
1714	Timaya Karwar	600	Mangalore to Congo, Ormuz
1714	King to Kanara	600	Mangalore to Congo, Ormuz
1714	King of Kanara	600	Basrur to Congo, Ormuz
1715	Abdul Razesh Karwar	1115	Karwar, Mangalore, Mecca
1715	King of Kanara	300	Basrur to Congo, Mecca
1715	King of Kanara	700	Basrur to Congo, Mecca
1716	Abdul Rasul Karwar	------	Mangalore to Mecca

1716	King of Kanara	716	Basrur to Congo, Bassora
1716	King of Kanara	700	Basrur to Congo, Bassora
1716	Sancarogi Naique	150	Basrur to Mecca Basrur
1716	Revadas Darmidas Mangalore	300	Mangalore to Mecca, Aden
1716	Sidha Raya Basrur	150	Basrur to Mecca
1716	Alue Xete Basrur	150	Basrur to Mecca
1717	Abdul Gafur Surat	600	Mangalore to Surat
1717	Sahide Taha Karwar	350	Mangalore to Congo
1717	Saida Mira Ankola	175	Karwar to Mangalore Aden
1717-18	Xeque Raxete Congo	-----	Mangalore to Congo
1718	King of Kanara	600	Basrur to Congo, Xerdufar
1718	King of Kanara	300	Basrur to Congo, Xerdufar
1718	Amadaxa Ankola	500	Karwar to Basrur Mangalore,
1719	Muve Xetty Basrur	150	Basrur to Mecca
1719	Sulu Naique Basrur	250	Basrur to Mecca
1721	King of Kanara	800	Ports of Kanara to Congo, ormuz
1721	King of Kanara	200	Ports of Kanara to Congo

1722	Abdul Razaca Mouso Ankola	500	Ankola to Mangalore, Mecca
1722	-----	800	Kanara ports to congo, Ormuz
1723	Amadax Mouso Ankola	500	Basrur to Ormuz, Congo
1724	Hamadaxa Cadir Perzada Ankola	350	Mangalore to Congo
1724	King of Kanara	1300	Basrur to Congo, Basora
1725	Hamadaxa Cadir Perzada Ankola	350	Honnavar Mangalore to Congo
1729	King of Kanara	300	Ports of Kanara to Bexadora, Congo, Ormuz, Bengal
1729	Sundardas Visttudas	600	Ports of Kanara to Baxadora, Congo, Ormuz, Bengal
1729	Sundardas Visttudas	600	Ports of Kanara to Baxadora, Congo, Ormuz, Bengal
1729	Gana Sinay Kundapur	175	Kundapur to Surat
1752	Bapaya Sinay	150	Kundapur to Muscat, Maldives
1754	Prenibaca Xety Guzarate	300	Calicut to Mangalore,

			Goa, Bombay, Damao, Surat, Diu, Muscat
1758	Ramachandra comotim Betim, Goa	55	Goa to Mangalore, Muscat

The above table shows that after 1700 the traders of South Kanara traded with Mecca, Congo, Surat, Bengal, Malabar and other regions. The volume of commodities was sometimes as high as 1500 *khandis*, which shows that the traders for sending goods to overseas destinations might have used large ships. Many outside traders started settling in the ports of South Kanara, particularly in Basrur. Gujarati and Telugu traders had their settlements in Basrur. Many of the *cartazes* were issued to merchants of Basrur. Gowda Saraswat Brahmins and Muslims were prominent among the merchants. A study of *Livro do Cartazes* shows that there was a gap between 1729 to 1752. This was the period when there were attack of Marathas and Arabs on the ports like Mangalore and Basrur. It is possible that due to political instability *cartazes* were perhaps not issued during this period.

The Dutch in South Kanara

During the beginning of the seventeenth century the Dutch started giving tough competition to the Portuguese in South Kanara.[102] The Dutch came to Barkur, Basrur and Mangalore, established their settlements and tried to get the supply of rice and pepper and more prominently rice to supply to their garrisons in Malabar. From the 1630s Dutch fleets made more regular appearances in Kanara. Kanara rice exports were also vital to the Dutch possessions in Srilanka. Thus under the Dutch the close connection between Kanara and Malabar that had existed under the Portuguese continued. Kanara merchant families got well-established in southern Malabar ports and entered into close links with the Dutch. The Dutch estimated that they could purchase about 12,50,000 pounds of pepper annually from Kanara, at prices which were about 25 to 50 per cent higher than in south Malabar. They decided to buy this pepper to avoid it falling into the hands of their European and Indian rivals. Also available in Kanara was abundant rice for Ceylon and Malabar. Kanara also supplied inferior cinnamon estimated at about 5,00,000 pounds. This too the Dutch wanted to prevent from falling into the hands of their European rivals.[103] The Dutch in the port of Vengurla procured rice from the ports of Kanara coast. The main item that was sent from the Konkan port of Vengurla to Ceylon was rice. It was the responsibility of the Vengurla factors to procure Kanara rice till 1670s when Dutch factories were established in the Kanara ports. There was a brisk rice trade carried on by Indian merchants from Kanara with places such as Muscat where the rate of gross profit earned in 1660 was reported to be 100 per cent. Some Kanara rice was occasionally also sent to Batavia.[104] In 1637 the Dutch entered into an alliance with Vasudeva, the Keladi administrator of Barkur. Vasudeva allowed the Dutch to establish a factory at Bokkapatna near Kalyanpur.[105] In 1660 a Dutch fleet came to Kanara for pepper trade. According to the orders from Joao Maetsukyar, the Viceroy of Batavia, Leen dert Leendertz, a sub-merchant proceeded to Basrur with letters to Venkatappa Nayaka and with a present of 100 nails, 140 nuts, 40 maces and 24 red clothes. The Dutch Governor Rykki Van der Dussen had also sent his treasurer from Colombo to collect 1500 loads of rice for the Dutch settlement in Ceylon. This was followed by the arrival of *De Gekoonds Leeuns* and *Elberg* and the yacht *De Starre* from Ceylon. These ships left Basrur for Batavia and Ceylon after securing freight.[106] Venkatappa Nayaka promised the Dutch to prohibit the Portuguese from buying rice on condition that the Dutch bought from Kanara all the rice available for export. But the Dutch were able to contract only for 1200 loads of rice at 13 Kanarese *pagodas*, a price that was considered high.[107] The Dutch had appointed Malik Mulla as their agent to carry rice to their destinations.[108]

In 1664 two Dutch ships arrived to capture Basrur and

Mangalore. They sent two of their ships to Mangalore and put up the Dutch colours on the walls, before the Portuguese took possession. But the local people resented this and they destroyed the flag. This shows that the traders of South Kanara had adjusted with the Portuguese traders and their practices.[109] Alexander Hamilton stated that the Dutch had a factory in Basrur to buy rice for their garrisons on the Malabar Coast.[110] Between 1663 and 1668 the Dutch were in ascendancy in Kanara and they established themselves in Kundapur and Mangalore.[111] In 1667 the Dutch entered into a treaty with the Nayaka of Ikkeri and were permitted to establish a factory in Basrur.[112] The Dutch were active in their factory at Basrur and they tried to monopolise rice trade. In May 1664, 102 vessels were filled with rice, coconuts, etc., for their settlements in the East.[113] Narayana Mallya, the court merchant of Bidanur was favourably disposed towards the Dutch. He made a representation on their behalf to the Bidanur court for removal of some of the tolls levied on their goods. They were able to get from Somashekhara Nayaka some concessions in Mangalore.[114] They contracted with the Nayaka to buy pepper at the market price, considerably higher than the Malabar price. The payment had to be made in cash as the Nayaka refused to accept payment in goods. In this factory the Dutch carried out purchases of pepper and rice, and were able to dispose of their imports such as spices and Japanese copper at Surat prices.[115] The Kanarese merchants replaced the old Malabar Hindu merchant groups who were not prepared to come to terms with the Dutch. According to S. Arasaratnam, the Kanara merchants were those who probably already had some role in the pepper trade in Malabar but who now became more prominent as middlemen and suppliers to the Dutch. They emerged as wholesale buyers and suppliers of pepper to the Dutch, and as buyers of Dutch imports such as spices, opium and Japanese copper. Through this means they drew closer to Dutch officials in Cochin and other ports, and mutually exchanged favours with them. They used their influence to carry on their commerce in the coastal trade in

Western and Eastern India. In Cochin the Kanara traders controlled the treasury, customs collection and the mint. The Raja of Cochin borrowed huge sums of loan from Kanara merchants.[116]

The Dutch consolidated their trade monopoly in Basrur. From Basrur they supplied rice to Malabar and assisted the pirates who worked against the English. Between 1738 and 1741 the Dutch in Basrur faced danger from the Marathas under Angrias of Kolaba. However the Dutch trade continued in Mulki.[117] In 1743 there was a Dutch Resident in the Mangalore fort. All foreign merchants had free trade with the people in Mangalore, Barkur and Mulki even though the contracts bestowed exclusive rights of trade to the Dutch East India Company. The Dutch Company had full monopoly of trade only in the port of Basrur.[118] Even as late as 1757 they had monopoly of rice trade at Basrur. But later they were completely eclipsed because of the increasing activities of the English on the one hand and the Marathas and Haidar Ali of Mysore on the other.[119]

The English Trade

The English were another European power that tried to challenge the Portuguese in South Kanara. In 1648 the English tried to sell coral in Basrur and Mangalore. These two ports were considered as the best places for the sale of coral.[120] According to Abbe Carre, the French agent Aubert joined the side of the English chief at Calicut and the latter appointed him to an agency under him at Mangalore.[121] In February 1687 the Surat Council stated that they were unable to supply rice to Bombay as provisions were dear and scarce everywhere. Thus Bombay had to acquire rice from Mangalore.[122]

Some of the political developments affected trade. It is said that the Kanara merchant Narna Mallo was responsible for the murder of the Keladi king and he fled from Keladi. In the absence of Narna Mallo trade was no longer carried out in Mangalore. The foreign merchants who formerly came to

European Factories in South Kanara

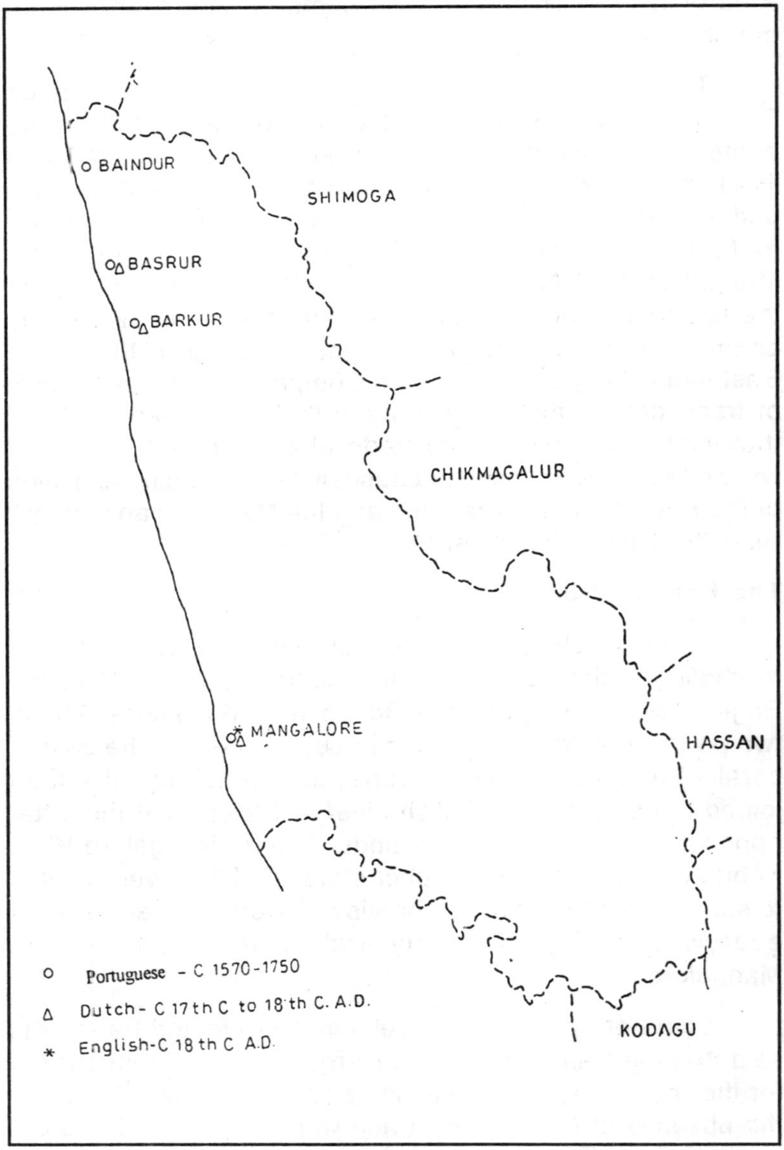

seek spices and merchandise would now go to the place to which Narna Mallo had fled, as the whole commerce and business of the kingdom were in his hands.[123] This only shows that trade was controlled by a few influential merchants, perhaps with the state support. One such trader was Narna Mallo, who had become very prominent in the commerce of South Kanara.

After 1715 the Keladi kings showed interest in capturing possessions in Malabar and this led them to conflict with the English. The English factors expressed anxiety about their grain supplies usually obtained through Mangalore.[124] In 1720 the English obtained 2500 bales of rice in Basrur.[125] Towards the close of January 1732, the region round about the river Valarpattanam also became unsettled due to the progress made by the Kanarese army. This meant starvation to the English settlements. There prevailed great anxiety with regard to the provision of grain for consumption in the ensuing monsoon season.[126] In May 1736 the English broke their relation with the Nayakas stating that the Company's broker at Mangalore had been fined and imprisoned on a false pretext.[127] A treaty was signed in February 1737 in which the Kanarese Governor of Mangalore, Surappaya, ratified all former grants to the Company and empowered the Company and their officers to export rice from Mangalore without paying the heavy duty called *adlamy*.[128] But later Somashekhara Nayaka refused to supply rice to the Company's vessels at Mangalore. By turning off the rice tap, Somashekhara had always in him power to inconvenience seriously the Company's settlements and to cause an artificial famine.[129]

The English document belonging to 1737 states that since rice supply did not arrive from Surat the English had to depend on the supply from Mangalore. It was decided that the English ships should stay in Mangalore port only for 15 days.[130] In 1737-38 the English decided to purchase 9,000 bales of rice at Mangalore at 23 *pagodas* per *corge*. The English were forced to sell their guns to the Kanarese in Mangalore in return for the sale of rice.[131] By March 1740 the English got from Mangalore 6,903 bales of rice and hoped to receive yet another 9,000 bales.[132] In 1740-41 the price of rice in Mangalore was 17½ pagodas per *corge*.[133] In 1741-42 rice was supplied from Mangalore to Tellicherry factory. In the same year the English agent Hur Commattee collected pepper from Mangalore to be sent to Tellicherry. This document states that the price of rice was 19 pagodas per corge.[134] In March 1741-42 the English ship loaded 4923 bales of rice and arrived at Tellicherry. A letter from Tellicherry states that on hearing that a small parcel of pepper was there at Mangalore they had sent 2900 Rupees, but one of the French servants bought it out of their hands at 32 *paggs*. and half the *candy* of 560 lb. and paid for it in Rupees at the rate of 373 per 100 *pagodas*. In the same year they received rice from Mangalore which was sufficient for their garrison for twelve months. The English tried to dispose of sword blades at Calicut, Mangalore and all adjacent parts but they could not get prime price for them.[135]

In 1743-44 the English decided to buy 20,000 *rubins* of rice from Mangalore.[136] Due to the scarcity of grain the English decided to prohibit exportation of grain from Bombay.[137] They contracted with Domingo Rodrigues for 12,000 bales of rice to be delivered in March (1744) allowing him 6 per cent on the Mangalore price with the usual charges of freight and package.[138] In March 1744 the Customs Master at Mangalore insisted that they should give the duty called *adlamy* which was 1 *pagoda* per *corge*. The English wanted to give only half a *pagoda* per *corge*. The English agent Cox had bought 20 *candies* of pepper at 27 *pagodas* and 10 *candies* at 26 *pagodas*.[139] In July 1744 the price of grain was 22½ rupees per *morah* of *batty*.[140] The English were forced to be friendly with the ruler of Bidanur. They could not afford to make the Keladi ruler angry since they depended on his territories for the supply of pepper and rice.[141] A letter from Tellicherry dated 18th November 1751 states that they had good fortune to receive rice from

Mangalore "or they had been driven to great streights" (*sic*).[142]

The above study shows that not only the Portuguese but also other Europeans like the Dutch and the English depended on the rice supplies from the ports of Kanara. The price of rice, pepper and other goods fluctuated from time to time. The political relations between the native kings and the European Companies determined the status of the supply of rice to European settlements. The naval ships were used to protect the goods carried by the European merchant ships from the pirates and the enemies.

Notes and References

1. Amiya Kumar Bagchi, 'Merchants and Colonialism', in D. N. Panigrahi (Ed.), ***Economy, Society and Politics in Modern India***, New Delhi, 1985, P. 3.

2. Sanjay Subrahmanyam, ***The Portuguese in Asia: A Political and Economic History,*** London, 1993, P.271 and P. 274.

3. *Ibid,* PP. 274-275.

4. *Ibid,* P. 106.

5. K. S. Mathew, ' Indian Merchants and the Portuguese Trade on the Malabar Coast during the Sixteenth Century', in Teotonio R. de Souza (Ed.), ***Indo-Portuguese History Old Issues, New Questions***, New Delhi, 1985, P.1.

6. Dietmar Rothermund, ***Asian Trade and European Expansion in the Age of Mercantilism***, Delhi, 1981, PP. 5-6.

7. J. C. Van Leur, ***Indonesian Trade and Society,*** The Hague, 1955, P. 118.

8. Niels Steensgard, ***Carracks, Caravans and Companies: The Structural Crisis in the European-Asian Trade in the Early 17th century,*** Copenhegen, 1972. PP. 81-114.

9. Sanjay Subrahmanyam, ***The Portuguese in Asia,*** *Op. Cit.*, P. 271.

10. *Ibid,* P. 274.

11. S. Arasaratnam, ***Maritime India in the Seventeenth Century***, *Op. Cit*, P. 194.

12. *Ibid*, P. 240.

13. *Ibid*, P. 223.

14. Sanjay Subrahmanyam, ***The Career and Legend of Vasco da Gama***, Cambridge University Press, 1997, P. 100.

15. B.Vasantha Shetty, "**Barakur- A Metropolitan City of Antiquity**", *Op. Cit.*, P. 215; H. Heras, ***The Aravidu Dynasty of Vijaynagara***, Vol.I., Madras, 1927; P. 59 .

16. B. S. Shastry, "**The Portuguese in Kanara 1498-1763**",*Op. Cit.*, PP. 68-69.

17. B. S. Shastry, 'Commercial Policy of the Portuguese in Coastal Karnataka', in H.V.Shrinivasamurthy *et.al.*,(Eds.), ***Essays On Indian History and Culture***, *Op. Cit.*, P.116.

18. H. Heras, *Op. Cit.*, P. 62.

19. S. Jayasheela Stephen, ***Portuguese in the Tamil Coast Historical Explorations in Commerce and Culture 1507-1749***, Pondicherry, 1998, P. 97; R. J. L. Felner, ***Subsidios Para a Historia da India Portuguesa***, Lisboa, 1868, P. 255.

20. John Sturrock, *Op. Cit.*, P. 69.

21. Edward Grey (Ed.), ***The Travels of Pietro Della Valle in India , Vol. II***, *Op. Cit.*, P. 320.

22. Teotonio R. de Souza, ***Medieval Goa***, New Delhi, 1979, PP. 34-35.

23. Sturrock, *Op.Cit.*, Vol. I, PP. 68-69.

24. K. D. Swaminathan, ***The Nayakas of Ikkeri***, *Op. Cit.*, P. 82.

25. B. S. Shastry, "**The Portuguese in Kanara 1498-1763**", *Op. Cit.*, P. 156.

26. *Ibid*, PP. 175-176.

27. *Ibid*, PP. 182-183.

28. *Ibid*, PP. 235-236; Biker J.F.J., ***Colleccao de Tratados e Concertos de Pazes***, Vol. IV, Lisbon, 1884, PP. 192-194.

29. B. S. Shastry, "**The Portuguese in Kanara 1498-1763**" *Op. Cit.*, PP. 240-242.

30. *Ibid,* PP. 244-245.

31. *Ibid,* P. 251-253.

32. Mansel Longworth Dames (Ed.), ***The Book of Duarte Barbosa...***, *Op. Cit,* P. 194.

33. *Ibid,* PP. 195-196.

34. *Ibid,* P. 196.

35. Genevieve Bouchon, ***'Regent of the Sea' Cannanore's Response to Portuguese Expansion, 1507-1528***, Delhi, 1998, P. 20; S. Arasaratnam, *Op. Cit.*, P. 108.

36. M.N. Pearson, ***Merchants and Rulers of Gujarat, The Response to the Portuguese in the Sixteenth Century***, New Delhi, 1976, PP. 46-47.

37. Celsa Pinto, ***Trade and Finance in Portuguese India A Study of the Portuguese Country Trade 1770-1840,*** New Delhi, 1994, P. 217.

38. Afzal Ahmad, ***Indo-Portuguese Trade in Seventeenth Century***,*Op. Cit.*, P. 116;S.Arasaratnam, *Op. Cit.*, P. 93.

39. A. R. Disney, ***Twilight of the Pepper Empire***,*Op. Cit.*, PP. 5-6.

40. B S. Shastry, **"The Portuguese in Kanara 1498-1763"**, *Op. Cit.,* P. 185.

41. *Ibid,* P. 218.

42. Afzal Ahmad, *Op. Cit.,* P. 117.

43. *Ibid,* P. 118.

44. *Ibid.*

45. Sanjay Subrahmanyam, 'The Portuguese, the Port of Basrur and Rice Trade 1600-1650', in *idem* (Ed.), ***Merchants, Markets and the State in Early Modern India***, *Op. Cit.*, P. 31.

46. *Ibid,* P. 34.

47. *Ibid,* P. 36.

48. ***Conselho do Fazenda*** (henceforth ***CDF), HAG***, 1627-31, fls. 89 v and 131 v. quoted in Sanjay Subrahmanyam, 'The Portuguese, the Port of Basrur and Rice Trade 1600-1650',*Op.Cit.,* P. 38.

49. ***CDF, HAG***, 1631-37, fl. 88 v., quoted in 'The Portuguese, the Port of Basrur and Rice Trade 1600-1650'*Op. Cit.,* P. 39.

50. ***CDF, HAG***, 1631-37, fls. 144-144v, 170 quoted in Sanjay Subrahmanyam, 'The Portuguese, the Port of Basrur and Rice Trade 1600-1650'*Op. Cit.,* P. 39.

51. Sanjay Subrahmanyam, 'The Portuguese, the Port of Basrur and Rice Trade 1600-1650',*Op.Cit,* P. 39.

52. *Ibid,* P. 40.

53. ***Afzal Ahmad,*** *Op. Cit.,* P. 121.

54. *Ibid,* P. 119.

55. *Ibid.*

56. A. R. Disney, *Op. Cit.,* PP. 36-38.

57. *Ibid,* P. 39.

58. *Ibid.*

59. *Ibid,* PP. 43-45.

60. *Ibid,* P. 104.

61. *Ibid,* P. 109

62. Afzal Ahmad, *Op. Cit.,* P. 78.

63. *Ibid,* P. 82.

64. *Ibid.*

65. S. Arasaratnam, *Op. Cit.,* PP. 93-94.

66. *Ibid,* P. 59.

67. Sanjay Subrahmanyam, 'The Portuguese, the Port of Basrur and Rice Trade 1600-1650' *Op. Cit.,* P. 32.

68. *Ibid,* P. 21.

69. *Ibid,* P. 37.

70. Afzal Ahmad, *Op. Cit.,* P. 10.

71. *Ibid,* P. 83.

72. *Ibid,* P. 85.

73. *Ibid,* P. 129.

74. B. Vasantha Shetty, ' A Keladi Copper plate from Kodladi (Kundapur Taluk)' in ***QJMS,*** Vol. LXXVIII, Issue No. 3-4, PP. 1-5.

75. Afzal Ahmad, *Op. Cit.,* P. 123.

76. B.S.Shastry, **"The Portuguese in Kanara 1498-1763"** *Op. Cit.,* P. 296.

77. Xavier Mariona Martins, **"Portuguese Shipping and Shipbuilding in Goa 1510-1780"**, Unpublished Ph.D. Thesis, Goa University, 1994, PP. 122-123.

78. *Ibid.*

79. B. S. Shastry, 'The Book of Correspondence Concerning Kanara: A Note', in, ***Indica,*** Volume 15, September, 1978, No. 2, PP. 121-126.

80. Alexander Hamilton, ***A New Account of the East Indies 1688-1723,*** Volume I, *Op. Cit.*, P. 281.

81. F. Y. Sousa, ***Decada da Asia,*** I, PP. 283-284.

82. *Ibid,* Vol. II, PP. 435-438.

83. B. S. Shastry, **"The Portuguese in Kanara 1498-1763"**, *Op. Cit.,* P. 115.

84. Sanjay Subrahmanyam, 'The Portuguese, the Port of Basrur and Rice Trade 1600-1650' *Op. Cit.,* P. 43.

85. K. G. Vasanthamadhava, 'Shivaji in Kanara and Contemporary Kannada Works', in, N.H.Kulkarni (Ed.), ***Chatrapati Shivaji Architect of Freedom,*** *Op. Cit.*, P. 152.

86. Alexander Hamilton, *Op. Cit.,* P. 283.

87. S. Arasaratnam, *Op. Cit.,* P. 199-200.

88. K.M.Mathew, **"Portuguese Navy in India 1498-1600"**, Unpublished Ph.D. Thesis, Bombay University, 1978, Appendix C-3.

89. B. S. Shastry, **"The Portuguese in Kanara 1498-1763"** *Op. Cit.,* PP. 110-111.

90. According to Sanjay Subrahmanyam, only those persons under the authority of the *Estado da India* could be termed *casados.* They had to be associated with a specific place of residence. In

Mangalore there existed the household of Christian converts, who can be termed as 'black *casados'*. In the official settlements of *Estado da India,* which were almost urban centres, physical space was organised in order to allow the *casados* to stay in one or several quarters. See Sanjay Subrahmanyam, ***The Portuguese Empire in Asia,*** *Op. Cit,* PP. 220-224.

91. B. S. Shastry, **"The Portuguese in Kanara 1498-1763"** *Op. Cit.,* PP. 100-102.

92. K. G. Vasanthamadhava, ***Trends in Karnataka Historical Research,*** *Op.Cit.*, P. 117.

93. Alexander Hamilton, *Op. Cit.,* P. 282.

94. Diogo do Couto quoted in Sanjay Subrahmanyam, *Op. Cit.,* PP. 30-31.

95. B. S.Shastry, 'Commercial Policy of the Portuguese in Coastal Karnataka: Sixteenth Century', *Op. Cit.,* P. 120.

96. Maria Augusta Lima Cruz, 'Notes on Portuguese Relations with Vijayanagara, 1500-1565', in Sanjay Subrahmanyam (Ed.), ***Sinners and Saints The Successors of Vasco da Gama***, New Delhi, 1998, P. 30.

97. A fee of Rs. 10 for every 100 *khandis* was charged at Mangalore in the 18th Century. In addition the charges of writers and other officials were also collected along with this fee. See, B. S. Shastry, **"The Portuguese inKanara 1498-1763"**, *Op. Cit.,* P. 305.

98. B. S. Shastry, 'Commercial Policy of the Portuguese in Coastal Karnataka: Sixteenth Century', *Op. Cit.,* P. 110.

99. *Ibid,* P. 111.

100. Sanjay Subrahmanyam (Ed), ***The Merchants, Markets and the State in Pre-Modern India,*** *Op. Cit.,* pp. 42-43.

101. ***Livro do Cartazes, HAG,*** Ms. 1363.

102. Teotonio R de Souza, ***Medieval Goa,*** *Op. Cit.*, P. 38.

103. S. Arasaratnam, *Op. Cit.,* P. 99

104. Om Prakash, 'The Dutch Factory at Vengurla in the Seventeenth Century', A.R. Kulkarni, M.A.Nayeem and T.R. de Souza (Ed.), ***Medieval Deccan History,*** Bombay, 1996, P. 189.

105. K. G. Vasanthamadhava, 'The Dutch in Coastal Karnataka 1602-

1763' in ***QJMS,*** Vol. LXXIII, July-December, 1982, Nos. 3 & 4, P. 2.

106. K. D. Swaminathan, *Op. Cit.*, P. 102.

107. ***Ibid,*** P. 103; ***Journal of Bombay Historical Society***, 1929, Vol. 2, PP. 248-249.

108. W.Foster, ***The English Factories in India, 1661-64,*** Oxford, 1923, P. 120.

109. George M. Moraes, ***Mangalore A Historical Sketch,*** *Op. Cit.*, P. 36.

110. Alexander Hamilton, *Op. Cit.*, P. 281.

111. Suryanath U. Kamath, 'Trade at Kannada Ports (1500-1800), in ***QJMS,*** July-December, 1980, P. 168.

112. S.Arasaratnam, *Op.Cit.,* P. 103.

113. ***Batavia Dagh Register,*** 1664, P. 448 quoted in K. D. Swaminathan, *Op. Cit.,* P. 113.

114. K. D. Swaminathan, *Op. Cit.,* PP 113-114.

115. S. Arasaratnam, *Op. Cit.,* P. 103.

116. *Ibid,* P.114 and P. 200.

117. K. G. Vasanthamadhava, 'The Dutch in Coastal Karnataka 1602-1763', *Op. Cit.,* P. 6.

118. George M. Moraes, *Op. Cit.,* P. 37.

119. K. G. Vasanthamadhava, 'The Dutch in Coastal Karnataka 1602-1763', *Op. Cit.,* P. 6.

120. William Foster, ***English Factories in India 1646-1650,*** Oxford, 1914, P. 199.

121. Fawcett (Ed.), ***The Travels of Abbe Carre in India and the Near East 1672 to 1674,*** Volume III, New Delhi, 1990, P. 696.

122. M.D.David, ***History of Bombay 1661-1708,*** Bombay, 1973, P. 398.

123. *Ibid,* PP. 697-700.

124. K. D. Swaminathan, *Op. Cit.,* P. 131.

125. ***Carwar Factory Outward Letter Book, 1720-22,*** No. 29A, No.2, P. 3.

126. K. D. Swaminathan, *Op. Cit.,* P. 131.

127. ***Public Department Diary***, 1737, No. 10 A, P. 160, Maharashtra State Archives, (henceforth MSA) Mumbai.

128. K. D. Swaminathan, *Op. Cit.*, PP. 135-136.

129. *Ibid*, P. 136.

130. ***Public Department Diary,*** MSA, No. 10 B/ 1737, P. 413.

131. ***Public Department Diary,*** MSA, No. 11 A/ 1738, P. 66.

132. ***Secretariat Inward Letter Book,*** MSA, No. 2/ 1740, P. 168.

133. ***Public Department Diary,*** MSA, No. 14 A/ 1740/41, P.118.

134. *Ibid*, No.15 A/ 1742, P. 42 and P. 85.

135. *Ibid*, P. 174, P. 210 and P. 211.

136. *Ibid*, No. 17 A/ 1744, P. 49.

137. *Ibid*, P. 50.

138. *Ibid*, P. 79.

139. *Ibid*, P. 147.

140. *Ibid*, No. 17 B/ 1744, P.244.

141. K. D. Swaminathan, *Op. Cit.*, P. 145.

142. ***Public Department Diary,*** No. 24 B/ 1751, P. 504.

7

Conclusion

This study on "Craft Production and Trade in South Kanara: A.D. 1000-1763" fills in a noticeable gap in the historiography of South Kanara, a region strategically located on the Western coast of Peninsular India. It is undertaken in the larger perspective of the economic history of medieval India. We have tapped both primary and secondary source materials in undertaking this study. Inscriptions, literary sources such as administrative records, foreign accounts, folklore, *kadatas* and published works in English, Portuguese and Kannada are extensively used. The introductory chapter provides the historical and historiographical backdrop to the present study. This study is both empirical and analytical in nature. While evidences are gathered from all possible sources, these evidences are analysed in the broader historical perspective with a comparative method by drawing parallels wherever possible.

From A.D. 1000 to 1763, South Kanara was ruled by different rulers like Alupas, Hoysalas, Vijayanagara and Keladi. Except the Alupas, all others had their political headquarters outside South Kanara. Political and administrative control of these powers on the peripheral region of South Kanara was relatively lesser. Nevertheless, these rulers showed considerable interest in safeguarding the polity and economy of South Kanara, for, it was economically important for them. South Kanara had several ports like Mangalore, Basrur, etc. and they played a dominant role in the promotion of trade. Besides the fall of Alupas saw the rise of several feudatory chieftains. For example, the Chautas of Ullal had become popular in the political history of the region due to their conflict with the Portuguese. These frequent changes in the politics of the region and lack of strong political rule had set the tune for much of the socio-economic developments in South Kanara.

The economy of South Kanara, as many other parts of India during the medieval period, depended primarily on agriculture. Industrial production or craft production was of secondary importance. Major industries like textiles, oil, coir, sugar, jaggery, etc. which existed during this period had to depend upon the primary sector for the raw materials. Other than these, there existed artisanal activities to a considerable extent. The tools and equipments required for agricultural and industrial production, utensils used in houses, ornaments, stone works, wood works and the like were produced. There was surplus production in agriculture and rice and pepper were exported in large quantities to other parts of India as also abroad. This was not applicable to industry where there was no much surplus production. Moreover, what existed in South Kanara was the domestic industry which was essential to the subsistence economy. The domestic industry and the flourishing agriculture largely co-existed and formed the two basic pillars of the economy of South Kanara. There was no much division of labour expressed in a separation of functions between food producers and artisans.

Our study reveals that there was migration of artisanal communities like Devangas, Padmasalis, etc. from other parts of India to South Kanara. Inscriptions and folk literature frequently refer to the artisanal activities. Textile production was a major industrial activity and it thrived in centres like Kavuru, Boluru, Basrur, Barkur, Baindur and Karkala. Another notable industrial activity was the production of salt. South Kanara was known for the cultivation of sugarcane and it was used in the manufacture of jaggery and sugar. However, references to sugar production are meagre. Jaggery was not only produced but also exported. Oil production, metal, wood and leather works, masonry, umbrella, hat and mat works were also carried out by artisans belonging to different communities. The society was caste-stratified and each of these activities was traditionally undertaken by the respective caste-people. The sources do not throw much light on the nature and composition of the industrial set up, level of technology and industrial production and distribution. On the basis of the sources consulted, it may not be wrong to say that the level and techniques of production were of traditional nature and did not develop well. The rulers did not show much interest in patronising the artisans and industries did not develop on par with agriculture.

It was chiefly due to the agrarian surplus that trade began and developed in South Kanara. Agrarian products like rice, coconut, arecanut, spices like pepper, cardamom, cinnamon, ginger, chilli, etc. were grown and exported to different destinations like Goa, Bombay, Malabar and to foreign ports like Muscat, Aden, etc. These items were also imported into South Kanara from the Western ghat region and the hinterland first, and then exported to places of demand. Cloth was imported even from far off places like Surat, Bombay and Cuddapah. Thus it was basically entrepot trade that thrived here. Ports like Basrur, Barkur and Mangalore acted as trans-shipment ports and entrepot trade ports. The rulers took keen interest in the promotion of agriculture and trade as they brought much revenues to the State. This trend developed more during the Vijayanagara and Keladi periods. Taxes were imposed on the shops. Transit and Custom duties were levied on goods involved in trade.

Due to the increased trading activity, trading centres emerged during this period. Udyavar, Barkur, Mangalore, etc. emerged as major centres of trade. The presence of itinerant traders was conspicuous. Besides them, many groups of local traders emerged. They generally belonged to the dominant Hindu group, namely, the Gowda Saraswat Brahmin caste. There were also Muslims, Jews and Jains who carried out trade. Foreign traders like Chinese, Arabs, Portuguese, English and the Dutch were also active in the mercantile activity of South Kanara. Their presence added new dimensions to the magnitude of trade. Some of these foreign traders entered into matrimonial alliances with the native women and thus strengthened their position to involve in active trade. The Arab traders got indigenised and settled in Kasargod, Kumbla, Mangalore, Mukka, Bhatkal and other coastal areas. They had contacts with their counterparts in Malabar. The Navayats were important traders who settled in places like Sirur, Baindur, Gangolli, Basrur, Hangarkatte, Malpe and so on. There were Indian trade centres in Arabia. The trade was both internal and external. Both these components were indispensable for the development of the economy.

The prevalence of exuberant trade is indicated by the existence of large number of trade or merchant guilds. Most prominent of them were *nakhara, settikara, hanjamana, elamegalu,* etc. They were quite active in the big trade centres. They not only protected their socio-economic interests, but also played the role of intermediaries in settling disputes, and had strong influence on the administration. They also caused the construction of temples, gave grants to religious institutions and managed the finances and lands of some of the temples. Their role as financiers or moneylenders is particularly notable. The heads of these guilds emerged as the new socio-economic elites. They played an important role in the socio-economic transformation of the region.

There was the emergence of urban centres like Basrur, Barkur and Mangalore. The town administrative system had evolved. Towns like Barkur and Basrur had several *keris.* Artisans who carried out different productive activities organised themselves and lived in their respective *keris.* Trade, religion and politics were the major factors in the process of urbanisation.

The existence of trade necessitated trade routes. There were land and sea routes used in inland and overseas trade respectively. South Kanara and its several busy ports were connected with the upghat regions through land routes. Similarly the rivers of this region facilitated inland trade. The ports facilitated foreign trade. The means of transport was primitive. In addition to human labour, bullock carts were used extensively in the transport of goods. In contrast to this the water transport system was more developed, particularly from the beginning of the 16th century thanks to the arrival of the Portuguese and other foreign ships. Native crafts were in use all over the coast from the ancient times onwards. The problem of piracy had to be faced by the sea traders and robbery was common on roads passing through the forests. Selection of quality wood and ship building developed as an art.

Apart from the urban centres and well developed commercial areas, there were regular fairs held daily or weekly in different parts of South Kanara. These fairs facilitated the exchange of goods between the local populace. The festivals held at religious institutions provided an opportunity for fairs and commercial centres like Subrahmanya, Dharmasthala, Udupi, etc. centred around these institutions had evolved.

The rulers issued coins of gold, silver and copper of different denominations from time to time. These were used in the process of exchange of goods. The barter system was also prevalent on a large scale.

The arrival of European traders in South Kanara during the sixteenth century and later was of great significance in the history of trade and commerce. The Portuguese, Dutch and the English traders were prominent. However, the Portuguese played a predominant role in the mercantile field. There was competition between the Portuguese and the Dutch in securing maximum merchandise from South Kanara. Later the English also joined them. The Portuguese were the first to represent Europe here as in India, and because their political headquarters in Goa was relatively closer to South Kanara, they were quite actively involved in trade. Further as Goa was a grain deficit region, they had to maintain close contact with the granary of the Western coast, namely, the Kanara region. Though they procured rice from the Konkan and Malabar areas, the import of Kanara rice was indispensable for Portuguese Goa. Of course they traded in spices like pepper, cardamom, etc. also. The Portuguese supplied horses to the Vijayanagara rulers. They entered into treaties with the Keladi rulers. These treaties had provisions relating to their political and commercial relations. When the Portuguese were able to impose their conditions on the weaker rulers of Keladi, the stronger rulers of Keladi resisted and they turned the table against the

Portuguese. They were able to assert themselves politically because they realised the Portuguese dependence on Kanara for rice, pepper and other goods. They could even bargain with the Portuguese for higher price. The Portuguese had issued *cartazes* to the merchants. Many Kanarese merchants held *cartazes* issued by them. The Portuguese had set up their fortress-factory system in the ports of South Kanara and they facilitated the growth of towns and provided a stimulus to urbanisation. They also promoted Christianity here. The arrival of the Dutch and English traders in addition to the Portuguese, increased the bargaining power of the Keladi rulers. The European factor in the Kanara trade favourably affected the economy of this region. There was favourable balance of trade. The quantum of merchandise increased by leaps and bounds. When there was increased demand, it acted as a catalyst in the area of agricultural production.

South Kanara from A.D. 1000 to 1763 saw the growth of craft production, agricultural production and trade. There was proliferation of artisanal communities and craft goods. New mercantile classes emerged. The economy of this region was linked with the rest of India and some other parts of the world. The economic condition presented pre-capitalist tendencies.

Appendix - 1
Muleya Svamya or Custom Duty in Saka Year 1304

Name of the item	**Duty**
100 *gadyanas* of the price of precious gems	2 panas
Bundle of camphor	1 haga
Pannekuru (perfume)	1 haga
One *tola* of musk	1 bile
One *nannu* of saffron	1 haga
One *tola* of *agilu* (fragrance)	½ adda
One *tola* of sandal	1 adda
Three *kanajus* of *sandhu* (fragrant substance)	1 haga
Three *kanajus* of civet	1 haga
Three *kanajus* of viverra civetta (punugu)	1 haga
One pair of Devagiri cloth	1 bile
One pair of marriage cloth	1 visa
One *malavi* of eighty bleached clothes	1 adda
One *tola* of silk yarn (*pattanulu*)	1 adda
One tola of silk cloth (dasari)	1 haga
One *malavi* of yarn	1 adda
One *malavi* of cotton	1 haga
One *malavi* of blankets	1 haga
One *kageya patte*	1 *visa*
One malavi of figured carpet	1 *haga*

One *malavi* of palmyra leaves	1 *haga*
One malvai of *patte* of sack	1 *haga*
Each load of paddy, jowat, raggy, navane, millet, save	1 bile
Per load of pulses : wheat, Bengal gram, sesamum, common flax (agase), green gram, uddu, togari, horse gram, etc.	1 haga
One manyadda ettu (bullock) coming from outside	1 haga
One load of oil and ghee	1 adda
One load of jaggery	1 haga
One load of sugar	1 adda
One load of arecanuts	1 haga
One load of betel leaves	1 haga
One load of black pepper	1 adda
One load of turmeric, onion, cumin seeds, box of fenugree, sabbasize, mustard, etc.	1 haga
One cart load of sugar-cane	1 haga
One load of green ginger	1 haga
One load of lime fruits	1 haga
One cart load of coconuts and vegetables	1 haga
One head-load of fruits, nuts and vegetables	1 haga
One cart load of timber	1 bile
One load of grass and fuel	1 bile
One gadyana of holeyakudre, khedileya kudure and nada kudure (horses)	1 bele
One gadyana of elephant	1 haga
One gadyana of camel	1 bele

One gadyana of tottiri (slaves)	1 bele
One gadyana of cart	1 bele
One ox	1 bele
One female buffalo	1 haga
One goat and sheep walking on foot	1 huluvisa

Ref: E.C., Volume IX, Belur, No. 171.

Appendix - II
Trade Guilds in the Inscriptions of South Kanara

Date (in Saka Year)	*Find spot*	*Inscription Number*	*Contents*
1256	Gurugala basti, Hiriyangadi	SII,VI, 310	Land grant given by nadu nakhara of Karkala to Shanthinathadeva basti constructed by samasta guddus of Karkala
1258	Mudukeri, Barkur	SII, VII, 312	Grant made by muvaru settikaras and nuraivattu elame at Murukeri
1282	Padmanabha Bhatta's house,	SII, VII, 329	Grant made by Naganna was not continued by Barkur his family. The halaru intervened and made them to continue the grant.
1312	Barkur	SII, VII, 353	Maintenance of a grant to the temple by manigara keriya muvaru settikararu nuraivattu elamegolagada samasta halaru.

1321	Barkur	SII, VII, 350	Reference to hattukeriya nakhara hanjamana of Barkur
Date less	Mudukeri, Barkur	SII, VII, 314	Arsanadu nakhar was asked to maintain landgrant.
1334	---do---	SII, VII, 310	Grant given to Lord Somanatha to be administered by halaru of Mudukeri.
1341	Kodiyal Bali near Mangalore	SII, VII, 182	Governor of Mangalore Timmanna Odeya attacked hanjamana nakhara who were given compensa tion by Bayicha Dannayaka.
Date less	---do---	SII, VII, 206	Role of yentu praje settikararu nalvaru elamegolagada samasta halaru in the construction of Tribhuvana chudamani.
1382	Hosabasti, Mudubidre	SII, VII, 200	Gift to tne temple with the consent of settikaras and halarus.
1384	---do---	SII, VII, 198	Land grant with the consent of yentu praje settikararu elamegolagada samasta halaru of Bidure nagara.
1385	Barkur	SII, VII,	Reference to to

		361	murukeriya halaru devasvada gadi
1387	---do---	SII, VII, 320	Reference to agrarian land owned by halaru
1398	Hosabasti, Mudubidre	SII, VII, 209	Construction of sandal wood structure in the middle of Tribhuvana chudamani by yentu mandi settikararu emlaeg-olagada samasta halaru of Bidure nagara.
1437	Mudubidre	SII, VII, 212	With the permission of yentu mandi settikararu nalvaru elamegolagada samasta halaru traders gave money donations
Date less	---do---	SII, VII, 213	Agreement among aruvaru ballalugalu yentu manisa settikararu nalvaru elamegalu eradu kola bali andnadu nakhar
1459	Shanthiswara basadi, Hiriyangadi	SII, VII, 256	Grant of land by hadinaru mandi settikararu munnura aruvattu mandi elamegalu
1464	Paduva Panambur, Mangalore taluk	SII, VII, 262	Brahmadaya with consent of yeradu nakharada samasta halaru.

1500	Bettakeri, Mudabidre	SII, VII, 226	With the permission of settikararu nalvaru elamegolgada samasta halaru it was decided that to the eastern side of Maindi Setti's house no houses should be constructed.

Ref: ***SII***, Volume, VII, Madras, 1986.

Appendix - III
Regimento De Barcelor

Designation	*Amount in Xerafins*
Capitao	400$000
Feitor	100$000
Escrivao da feitoria	50$000
Ouvidor	60$000
Meirinho	18$000
Escrivao do meirinho	12$000
Fisico e cirurgiao	30$000
Condestavel	46$000
Porteiro	$600
Lingua ou interprete	1$200
Vigario da Igrez	30$000
Tesoureiro da igreja	6$000

Source: Antonio da Silva Rego, **Documentacao Para A Historia Das Missões do Padroado Portuguêse Do Oriente,** Vol. 9, (1562-1565), Lisboa, 1953, P. 588

Appendix - IV
Regimento De Barcelor

Designation	Amount in *Xerafins*
Meirinho	18$000
Escrivao do feitoria	40$000
Escrivao do meirinho	12$000
Condestavel	24$000
Lingua ou interprete da fortaleza	1$200

Source: Antonio da Silva Rego, **Documentacao Para A Historia Das Missões do Padroado Portuguêse Do Oriente,** Vol. 9, (1562-1565), Lisboa, 1953, P. 588

Appendix - V

Despesas Da fortalezas	*Amount in Xerafins*
Onor	1$406-3-00
Cambolim	1$184-0-00
Barcelor	1$256-1-40
Mangalor	$761.3-40

Source: A. B. de Braganca Pereira (Ed.), Arquivo Português Oriental, Tomo IV, Vol. II, 1600=1699, Parte I, Bastora, 1937, P.V.

Appendix - VI

Transcript of the paper which the chief, Mr. William Wake, gave to the Governor, SURAPAYA, on the 18th February 1739-40 on the final settlement of the peace, which was effected between the king of Canara and the Honourable Company.

Notwithstanding it is stipulated in the 5th Article of Agreement entered into between the King of Bidnure and the Honourable Company, February the sixteenth, one thousand seven hundred thirty six-seven, that the Manchuas employed by them, the President of Bombay, Chief of Tellicherry, their officers here and at Calicut, trading to the Canara ports, shall be exempted from paying the duty called Adlamy on rice exported thereform. It is hereby now agreed that the quantity of three hundred corge of rice of forty-two bales, provided annually in any of the Carnatic ports for the use of Tellicherry settlement, on the Honourable United English East India Company's account, shall be exempt from the duty called Adlamy; but whatever rice is further laden in any of the aforesaid ports by the said Company, their servants, officers and others, under their protection at Tellicherry and Calicut, on board any vessel carrying English colours shall be liable to the duty of half pagoda per corge.

Dated in Tellicherry, this eighteenth day of February, one thousand seven hundred and thirty nine-forty.

Source: William Logan (Ed.), ***A Collectiuon of Treaties, Engagements and other Paper of Importance Relating To British Affairs in Malabar, Malabar Manual,*** Vol. III, Reprint, 1998, Madras, P.40

Bibliography

(I) **PRIMARY SOURCES:**

(A) **INSCRIPTIONS:**

Annual Report of South Indian Epigraphy, 1900-1954.

Aiyar, K. V. Subrahmanya (Ed.), ***South-Indian Inscriptions Volume VII,***

Miscellaneous Inscriptions in Tamil, Malayalam, Telugu and Kannada, The Director (Epigraphy), Mysore, 1986.

Epigraphia Carnatica, Volume VIII, Inscriptions of the Shimoga District, Part II, Mysore, 1904.

Epigraphia Carnatica, New Series.

Epigraphia Indica

Indian Antiquary

Mysore Archaeological Report, Archaeological Survey of India, Mysore.

Ramesh, K.V. (Ed.), ***Tulunadina Shasanagalu*** (in Kannada), Geeta Book House Mysore, 1978.

Rice, Lewis, ***Mysore and Coorg from Inscriptions,*** Vol. II, London, 1909.

Sastry, R. Shama and N. Lakshminarayan Rao,(Eds.), ***South-Indian Inscriptions (Texts) Volume IX-Part II, Kannada Inscriptions From the Madras Presidency,*** The Director (Epigraphy), Mysore, 1986.

Panchamukhi, R.S. (Ed.), ***Karnataka Inscriptions,*** Karnatak University, Dharwar, 1941.

(B) ARCHIVAL SOURCES

Carwar Factory Outward Letter Book, No. 29 A, 1720-22, ***Maharashtra State Archives.***

Conselho da Fazenda, Historical Archives of Goa.

Kadatas (account books) ***in the collections of K. G. Vasanthamadhava, Pavanje and Munjunatha Shenoy, Gangolli.***

Livro do Cartazes (Book of Sailing Permits), ***Historical Archives of Goa,*** Ms. No. 1363.

Livro do Correspondencia do Kanara, 2 Volumes, ***Historical Archives of Goa,*** Ms. No. 1372 and Ms. No. 1373.

Public Department Diary, No. 10 A, 1737, No. 10 B, 1738, No. 14 A, 1740- 41, No. 15 A, 1742, No. A, 1744, No. 17 B, 1744, No. 24 B, 1751

Maharashtra State Archives.

Secretariat Inward Letter Book, No. 2, 1740, ***Maharashtra State Archives.***

(C) PUBLISHED PORTUGUESE BOOKS

Biker, J.F.Judice (Ed.), ***Collecção de Tratados e Concertos de Pazes que o Estado da Índia Portugueza fez com os Reis e Senhores com quem teve relações nas Partes da Asia e Africa Orietnal desde o Principio da Conquista até ao fim do Seculo XVIII,*** (in 14 *Tomos*)

(Collection of Treaties and Agreements), Lisboa, 1881-1887.,14 Volumes, Lisbon, 1881-1887.

Felner, R.J.C. de Lima (Ed.), ***Década 13 da História da India,*** 2 Volumes, Academia Real das Ciencias, Lisbon, 1876.

Felner, R.J.C. de Lima (Ed.), ***Subsidíos para a História da Índia Portugueza,*** Academia Real das Ciencias, Lisbon, 1868.

Pereira, A.B. de Bragança (Ed.), ***Arquivo Português Oriental,*** *Tomo* IV, Volume II, 1600-1699, *Parte* I, Bastora, 1937.

Pissurlencar, P.S.S. (Ed.), ***Regimentos das Fortalezas da Índia,*** Goa, 1951.

———, ***Assentos do Conselho do Estado***(1618-1750), 5 Volumes, Goa, 1953-1957.

Rego, A. da Silva (Ed.), ***Documentação Para a História das Missoes do Padroado Português do Orient India, (1499-1582),*** Agencia Geral das Colonias do Ultramar, 12 Volumes, Lisbon, 1947-1958.

Silveira, Luiz da, ***Livro das Plantas Fortalezas, Cidades e Provoações do Estado da India Oriental, com as Descrições do Maritimo dos Reinos e Provincias onde estão Situados e outros Portos Principais daqueles partes, Contrinuição para a Historia das Fortalezas dos Portugueses no ultramar,*** Lisboa, 1991.

(II) TRAVELOGUES

Buchanan, H. Francis, ***Journey From Madras Through the Countries of Mysore, Canara and Malabar,*** in 3 volumes, Asian Educational Services, Madras, 1989.

Burnell, Arthur Coke (Ed.), ***The Voyage of John Huyghen Van Linschoten to the East Indies,*** Asian Educational Services, New Delhi, 1988.

Cortesao, Armando, (Ed.), ***The Suma Oriental of Tom Pires,*** Asian Educational Services, New Delhi, 1990.

Fawcett (Ed.), ***The Travels of Abbe Carre in India and the Near East 1672 to 1674,*** Volume III, Asian Educational Services, New Delhi, 1990.

Gibb, H.A.R. (Translated and Selected), ***Ibn Batuta Travels in Asia and Africa 1325-1354,*** Asian Educational Services, New Delhi, 1992.

Gowda, H.L. Nage, (Ed.), ***Pravasi Kanda India,*** Volumes II- VI, Prasaranga, Mysore University, Mysore, 1966-1977.

Grey, Edward, (Ed.), ***The Travels of Pietro Della Valle in India, Volume II***, Asian Educational Services, New Delhi, 1991.

Hamilton, Alexander, ***A New Account of the East Indies, 1688-1723, Volume I,*** Asian Educational Services, Madras, 1995.

Longworth, Mansel, (Ed.), ***The Book of Duarte Barbosa,*** Asian Educational Services, New Delhi, 1989.

Varthema, Ludovico de, ***Itinerario,*** Lisboa, 1949, Milan, 1956.

(III) UNPUBLISHED PH.D. THESES, M PHIL. DISSERTATION AND PROJECT REPORTS

Bai, U. Shaila, **Dakshina Kannada Jilleya Shasanagala Samskrutika Adhyayana**, (in Kannada), Ph.D. Thesis, Mangalore University, 1998.

Bari, Syed Abdul, **Non Agrarian Taxation in Karnataka under Vijayanagara (1336-1565)**, Ph.D. Thesis, Mangalore University, 1988.

Kamath, U. Suryanath, **Tuluva in the Vijayanagara Times 1336-1646**, Ph.D. Thesis, Bombay, 1965.

Martins, Xavier M., **Portuguese Shipbuilding in Goa 1510-1780**, Ph.D. Thesis, Goa University, 1994.

Mathew, K.M., **Portuguese Navy in India 1498-1600**, Ph.D. Thesis, Bombay University,1978.

Murthy, K. Malathi, **Trade and Commerce in Colonial South Kanara (1799-1862)**, Ph.D. Thesis, Mangalore University, 1991.

Murthy, P.N. Narasimha, **Jainism on the Kanara Coast,** Ph.D. Thesis, Mysore University, 1983.

Rao, Nagendra, **The Historical Tradition of South Canara and the Brahmanical Groups: A Study of *Gramapaddhati* and *Sahyadri Khanda***, M.Phil. Dissertation, Mangalore University, 1995.

---------,**Urbanization in Western Coastal India 1336-1763,** Minor Research Project Report, Goa University, 2000.

Shastry, B.S., **The Portuguese in Kanara 1498-1763**, Ph.D. Thesis, Bombay University,1969.

Shastry, A.K., **Selections From the Kaditas of the Sringeri Matha**, ICHR Project Report, 1982.

Shetty, B. Jagadish, **The Agro-Economic Relations and Social Structure in Dakshina Kannada (A.D. 1000-1600)**, Ph.D. Thesis, Mangalore University,1992.

Shetty, B. Vasantha, **Barakuru-A Metropolitan City of Antiquity,** Ph.D. Thesis, Mysore University, 1985.

Vasanthamadhava, K.G., **Political History of Kanara 1565-1763 (A Study mainly based on Inscriptions)**, Ph.D. Thesis, Karnatak University, Dharwar, 1977.

(IV) ARTICLES FROM JOURNALS

De Souza, 'Mhamai House Records: Indigenous Sources for Indo-Portuguese Historiography', ***The Indian Archives,*** No. 1.Volume XXXI, anuary-June 1982.

Fischel, W.J., 'The Spice Trade in Mamluk Egypt, A Contribution to the Economic History of Medieval Islam', ***JESHO,*** Number 1, 1958.

Gowda, Ho. Na. Nilakantha and M. G. Manjunatha, Mudabidare Jaina Mathada Aprakatita Jaina Shasanagalu' (in Kannada), ***Itihasa Darshana,*** Volume 14, Karnataka Itihasa Academy, Bangalore, 1995.

Haynes, E. Douglas and Tirthankar Roy, 'Conceiving Mobility: weaver's migrations in pre-colonial and colonial India', ***IESHR,*** XXXVI, Number 1, January-March, 1999.

Kamath, U. Suryanath, 'Hanjamana', in ***The Journal of Institute of Asian Studies,*** Volume 1, Number 1, May 1978.

-------, 'Trade at Kannada Ports (1500-1800)', in ***QJMS,*** No. July-December, 1980.

Moraes, M. George, ' Haryab of Ibn Batuta' in ***Journal of Bombay Branch of Royal Asiatic Society***, N.S. Volume 15.

Perlin, Frank (Ed.), 'Proto-industrialization and pre-colonial south Asia', ***Past and Present,*** Volume XCVIII, 1983.

Ramaswamy, Vijaya, 'Artisans in Vijayanagara Society', in ***IESHR,*** Volume XXII, Number 4, 1985.

Shastry, B.S., 'The Book of Correspondence Concerning Kanara: A Note', in ***Indica,*** Volume 15, September, 1978.

Shetty, B. Vasantha, 'A Keladi Copper plate from Kodladi (Kundapur Taluk)', in ***QJMS***, LXXVIII, Issue Number, 3-4.

Spencer, W.George, 'Temple Money-Lending and Livestock Redistribution', ***IESHR,*** Volume 5, Number 3, 1968.

Vasanthamadhava, K.G., 'The Dutch in Coastal Karnataka', in ***QJMS,*** LXXIII, July-December, 1982, Numbers 3 & 4.

------'Karavali Karnataka Nanyagalu',(in Kannada) in ***Satya Shuddha Kayaka,*** Volume 2, Number 5-6, May-August, 1992.

------ 'Baindurina Eradu Shilashasanagala Adhyayana', (in Kannada) in ***Itihasa Darshana,*** Volume 14, Karnataka Itihasa Academy, Bangalore, 1995.

—,'Karnataka's Trade with the Arab World (c. 9th to 19th C. A.D.), ***QRHS,*** XXXVI, Numbers 1 & 2, April-September, 1996.

(V) BOOKS

(A) ENGLISH

Abraham, Meera, ***Two Medieval Merchant Guilds of South India,*** Manohar, Delhi, 1988.

Ahmad, Afzal, ***Indo Portuguese Trade in the Seventeenth Century,*** Gian Publishing House, New Delhi, 1991.

Arasaratnam, Sinnappah, ***Merchants, Companies and Commerce on the Coromandel Coast 1650-1740,*** Oxford University Press, Delhi, 1986.

Arasaratnam, Sinnappah, ***Maritime India in the Seventeenth Century,*** Oxford University Press, Delhi, 1997.

Banga, Indu,(Ed.), ***Ports and their Hinterlands in India 1700-1950***, Manohar, New Delhi, 1992.

Birdwood, G.C.M., ***The Arts of India,*** Rupa & Co., Bombay, 1994.

Bhat, N. Shyam, ***South Kanara 1799-1860: A Study in Colonial Administration and Regional Response,*** Mittal, New Delhi, 1998.

Bhatt, P. Gururaja, ***Antiquities of South Kanara,*** Udupi, 1969.

-----,***Studies in Tuluva History and Culture,*** Kallianpur, 1975.

Bouchon, Genevieve, ***'Regent of the Sea', Cannanore's Response to Portuguese Expansion, 1507-1528,*** Delhi, 1998.

Champakalakshmi, R., ***Trade, Ideology and Urbanization South India 300 B.C. – A.D. 1300,*** Oxford University Press, Delhi, 1996.

Cambell, M. James, ***Gazetteer of the Bombay Presidency, Volume XV, Part I, Kanara,*** Government Press, Bombay, 1885.

Chaudhuri, K.N., ***Asia Before Europe: Economy and Civilization of the Indian Ocean From the Rise of Islam to 1750,*** Cambridge University Press, Cambridge, 1990.

Chitnis, K.N., ***Keladi Polity,*** Karnatak University, Dharwar, 1974.

Danvers, F.C., ***Report on the Portuguese Records Relating to the East Indies***, Asian Educational Services, New Delhi, 1991.

David, M.D., ***History of Bombay 1661-1708,*** Bombay, 1977.

D' Souza, S. Victor, ***The Navayats of Kanara A Study in Culture Contact,*** Karnatak University, Dharwar, 1955.

De Souza, R. Teotonio, ***Medieval Goa,*** New Delhi, 1979.

De Souza, R. Teotonio, ***Indo-Portuguese History Old Issues, New Questions***, Concept Publishing Company, New Delhi, 1984.

Dikshit, G.S. (Ed.), ***Studies in Keladi History,*** Mythic Society, Bangalore, 1981.

Disney, A.R., ***Twilight of the Pepper Empire, Portuguese Trade in South West India in the Early Seventeenth Century,*** Cambridge University Press, Cambridge, 1978.

Fleet, John Faithfull, ***Dynasties of the Kanarese Districts,*** Asian Educational Services, New Delhi, 1988.

Foster, W. (Ed.), ***The English Factories in India 1618-1669,*** 13 Volumes, Oxford, 1906-1927.

Goitein, S.D., ***Letters of Jewish Traders,*** Princeton University Press, Princeton, 1972.

Gopal, Surendra, ***Commerce and Crafts in Gujarat 16th and 17th Centuries: A Study of the Impact of European Expansion and Pre Capitalist Economy,*** New Delhi, 1975.

Gupta, D.N. (Ed.), ***Changing Modes of Production in India An Historical Analysis,*** Hindu College, Delhi, 1995.

Gururajachar, S., ***Some Aspects of Economic and Social Life in Karnataka, A.D.1000-1300,*** Prasaranga, University of Mysore, 1974.

Jain, V.K., ***Trade and Traders in Western India (A.D. 1000-1300)***, New Delhi, 1990.

Hall, R. Kenneth, ***Trade and Statecraft in the Age of Colas,*** Abhinav Publications, New Delhi, 1980.

Heras, Henry, ***The Aravidu Dynasty of Vijayanagara,*** Volume I, Poona, 1936.

Hietzman, James, ***The Gifts of Power Lordship in an Early Indian State,*** Oxford University Press, New Delhi, 1997.

Kulkarni, A.R., M.A.Nayeem and T.R. de Souza (Eds.), ***Mediaeval Deccan History Commemoration Volume in Honour of P.M. Joshi***, Popular Prakashan, Bombay, 1996.

Kulkarni, N.H. (Ed.), ***Chatrapati Architect of Freedom,*** New Delhi, 1973.

Kuppuswamy, G.R., ***Economic Conditions in Karnataka (A.D. 973-A.D. 1336),*** Karnatak University, Dharwar, 1975.

Leur, Van J.C., ***Indonesian Trade And Society,*** The Hague, 1955.

Logan, William (Ed.), ***A Collection of Treaties, Engagements and other Papers of Importance Relating To British Affairs in Malabar,Malabar Manual,*** Volume III, Reprint 1998.

Lombard, Denys and Jean Aubin (Eds.), ***Asian Merchants and Businessmen in the Indian Ocean and the China Sea,*** Oxford University Press, New Delhi, 2000.

Mahalingam, T.V., ***Administration and Social Life under Vijayanagara Part II: Social Life,*** Madras University, Madras, 1975.

Mathew, K.S. (Ed.), ***Mariners, Merchants and Oceans Studies in Maritime History,*** Manohar, Delhi, 1995.

Moraes, George M. , ***Mangalore: A Historical Sketch,*** Mangalore, 1927.

Murthy, H.V.Sreenivasa, *et.al.*, (Eds.) ***Essays on Indian History and Culture (Felicitation Volume in Honour of Prof. B.Sheikh Ali),*** Mittal Publications, New Delhi, 1990.

Nainar S, Muhammad Husayn, (Ed.), ***The Knowledge of India Possessed by Arab Geographers Down To 14th Century A.D. with Special Reference to Southern India,*** Madras, 1942.

Panigrahi, D.N. (Ed.), ***Economy, Society and Politics in Modern India,*** New Delhi, 1985.

Pearson, M.N., ***Merchants and Rulers of Gujarat, the Response to the Portuguese in the Sixteenth Century,*** New Delhi, 1976.

Pearson, M.N., ***Coastal Western India: Studies from the Portuguese Records,*** Concept Publishing Company, New Delhi, 1981.

Pinto, Celsa, ***Trade and Finance in Portuguese India A Study of the Portuguese Country Trade, 1770-1840,*** New Delhi, 1994.

Prakash, Om, ***The Dutch East India Company and the Economy of Bengal, 1630-1720,*** Princeton University Press, Princeton, 1985.

------, ***The New Cambridge History of India Volume II.5, European Commercial Enterprise in Pre-Colonial India,*** Cambridge University Press, Cambridge, 1998.

Prasad, Om Prakash, ***Decay and Revival of Urban Centres in Medieval South India (A.D. 600-1200),*** Janaki Prakashan, Patna, 1989.

Ramaswamy, Vijaya, ***Textiles and Weavers in Medieval South India,*** Delhi, 1985.

Ramesh, K.V., ***A History of South Kanara (From earliest times to the fall of Vijayanagara),*** Karnatak University, Dharwar, 1970.

Rao, S.R. (Ed.), ***The Role of Universities And Research Institutes in Marine Archaeology,*** Goa, 1994.

Rao, S.R. (Ed.), ***An Intergrated Approach to Marine Archaeology,*** Goa, 1997.

Rayachaudhuri, Tapan and Irfan Habib (Eds.), ***The Cambridge Economic History of India***, Volume I, Cambridge University Press, Cambridge, 1982.

Rothermund, Dietmar, ***Asian Trade and European Expansion in the Age of Mercantilism,*** Manohar, Delhi, 1981.

Saletore, B.A., ***Ancient Karnataka, Volume I, History of Tuluva,*** Oriental Book Agency, Poona, 1936.

Saletore, R.N., ***Indian Pirates,*** Delhi, 1978.

Saradaraju, A, ***Economic Conditions in the Madras Presidency 1800-1850,*** Madras, 1941.

Sharma, R.S., ***Indian Feudalism : c. 300-1200,*** Calcutta, 1965.

Shastry, B.S., ***Studies in Indo-Portuguese History,*** IBH Prakashana, Bangalore, 1981.

Sewell, Robert, ***A Forgotten Empire (Vijayanagar) A Contribution to the History of India,*** Asian Educational Services, New Delhi, 1992.

Steensgard, Niels, ***Carracks, Caravans and Companies: The Structural Crisis in the European-Asian Trade in the Early 17th Century,*** Copenhegen, 1972.

Stein, Burton, ***The New Cambridge History of India, Vijayanagara,*** Cambridge University Press, Cambridge, 1989.

Stephen, S. Jayasheela, ***The Coromandel Coast and its Hinterland Economy, Society and Political System (A.D. 1500-1600),*** Manohar, Delhi, 1997.

Shivanna, K.S., ***The Agrarian System of Karnataka (1336-1761),*** University of Mysore, 1983.

Stuart, H.A., ***Madras District Manuals, South Kanara Volume II,*** Government Press, Madras, 1895.

Stein, Burton, ***The Making of Agrarian Policy in British***

India 1770-1900, Oxford University Press, Delhi, 1992.

Sturrock, John, ***Madras District Manuals, South Kanara, Volume I,*** Government Press, Madras, 1894.

Subrahmanyam, Sanjay (Ed.), ***Merchants, Markets and State in Early Modern India,*** Delhi, 1990.

------,***The Political Economy of Commerce: Southern India 1500-1650,*** Cambridge University Press, Cambridge, 1990.

------,(Ed.), ***Money and Market India, 1100-1700,*** Oxford University Press, Delhi, 1994.

------, ***The Career and Legend of Vasco da Gama,*** Cam bridge University Press, Cambridge, 1997.

------ (Ed.), ***Sinners and Saints The Successors of Vasco da Gama,*** Oxford University Press, New Delhi, 1998.

Swaminathan, K.D., ***The Nayakas of Ikkeri,*** Madras, 1957.

Tchitcherov, I. Alexander, ***Changing Economic Structure in the Sixteenth-Eighteenth Centuries Outline History of Crafts and Trade,*** Manohar, Delhi, 1998.

Thakur, Vijay Kumar (Ed.), ***Towns in Pre-Modern India,*** Janaki Prakashan, Patna, 1994.

Thapar, Romila, ***From Lineage to State: Social Formations in the Mid-First Millennium B.C. in the Ganga Valley,*** New Delhi, 1990.

Vasanthamadhava, K.G., ***Western Karnataka Its Agrarian Relations 1500-1800,*** Navrang, New Delhi, 1991.

-----, ***Trends in Karnataka Historical Research,*** Mangalore, 1996.

Veluthat, Kesavan, ***Brahman Settlements in Kerala: Historical Studies,*** Calicut, 1978.

Venkataratnam, A.V., ***Local Government in the Vijayanagara Empire,*** Mysore University, Mysore, 1972.

Viratappa, K. (Ed.), ***Studies in Karnataka History and Culture,*** Proceedings Volume II, Karnataka History Congress, Mysore, 1987.

(B) **KANNADA**

Achar, Paltadi Ramakrishna. ***Kalkuda Kallurti Samskriti Shodha,*** Puttur, 1998.

Aigal, M. Ganapathi Rao, ***Dakshina Kannada Jilleya Prachina Itihasa,*** Mangalore, 1923.

Annigeri, A.M., (Translated), ***Nanyagalu,*** Karnatak University, 1992.

Bhat, Heranje Krishna (Ed.), ***Govinda Pai Samshodhana Samputa,*** Rashtra Kavi Govinda Pai Samshodhana Kendra Udupi, Manipal, 1995.

Bhat, K. Vadiraja, ***Paddanagalu,*** Yugapurusha Prakatanalaya, Kinnigoli, 1974.

Bhatta, Adyanadka Krishna (Ed.), ***Sudarshana,*** Mulki, 1977.

Chandrashekhar, (Ed.), ***Gomateswara Charitre,*** Government Press, Madras, 1951.

Jois, K.G. Venkatesh, ***Keladi Shasanagala Samskruthika Adhyayana,*** Kannada Sahitya Prishat, Bangalore, 1996.

Murthy, A.V. Narasimha, ***Vijayanagarada Nanya Sampattu,*** Mysore University, Mysore, 1996.

Pinto, Pius Phidelis, ***Karavali Karnatakada Kraistara Itihasa (1500-1763),*** Samanvaya Prakashana, Mangalore, 1999.

Manipal, Arke, ***Hesarinallenide?,*** New Star Publications, Bangalore, 1989.

Rai, A. Subbanna, ***Da. Ka. Jilleya Aitihyagalu,*** Bombay, 1994.

Rai, B.A. Vivek, ***Tuluva Adhyayana: Kelavu Vicharagalu,*** Tuluva Prakashana, Mangalore, 1980.

------, ***Tulu Janapada Sahitya,*** Kannada Sahitya Parishat, Bangalore, 1985.

Ramesh, K.V., ***Tulunadina Itihasa,*** Geeta Book House, Mysore 1969.

Ramesh, K.V., and M.J. Sharma, ***Tulunadina Arasumanetanagalu,*** Shree Manjunatheshwara Pustaka Prakashana Male, Ujire, 1985.

Sastri, R. Shama, ***Linganna Kavi Virachita Keladi Nripa Vijayam,*** Institute of Kannada Studies, Mysore University, Mysore, 1973.

Shastry, B.S., ***Keladiya Arasaru Hagoo Portuguesaru,*** Karnatak University, Dharwad, 1972.

Shenoy, Y. Umanath, ***Karkalada Sri Gomateshwara Charitre,*** Ujire, 1991.

------, ***Manjuvani,*** Dharmasthala, 1989.

Silva, S, ***Mangalore,*** Ankola, 1956.

Someshwara, Amrita (Ed.), ***Tulu Paddana Samputa,*** Kannada University, Hampi, 1997.

Upadhyaya, B. Laxminarayana (Ed.), ***Hesarada Pattana Basruru Ondu Adhyayana,*** Basrur, 1997.

Vasanthamadhava, K.G., ***Karavali Karnatakada Rajakiya Itihasa Adhyayana Mattu Samshodhane,*** Nammi-Ananta Prakashana Haleyangadi, 1998.

Index

F

G

H

I